The Private Practice
of
Psychotherapy

The Private Practice of Psychotherapy

ARNOLD M. LEVIN

THE FREE PRESS
A Division of Macmillan, Inc.
NEW YORK

Collier Macmillan Publishers
LONDON

The Free Press
A Division of Macmillan, Inc.
866 Third Avenue, New York, N.Y. 10022

Collier Macmillan Canada, Inc.

Printed in the United States of America

printing number
1 2 3 4 5 6 7 8 9 10

Library of Congress Cataloging in Publication Data

Levin, Arnold M.
   The private practice of psychotherapy.

   Bibliography: p.
   Includes index.
   1. Psychotherapy—Practice.   I. Title.   [DNLM:
1. Psychotherapy.   2. Private practice.   WM 21 L665p]
RC480.5.L47   616.89'14   83-47789
ISBN 0-02-918830-X

Table 6.3 (pp. 108–109) is reproduced courtesy of American Professional
Agency, Inc., 95 Broadway, Amityville, NY 11701—(516) 691-6400.

Tables 7.1 (p. 155) and 7.2 (p. 157) are reproduced courtesy of Atcom, Inc.,
Publishers, Atcom Bldg., 2315 Broadway, New York, NY 10024

This book is dedicated with love to my three children: Michael, Nancy and Amy; to the memory of their late mother, Elaine Z. Levin; to Mrs. Terry Levin and Mr. John Noteman; and to my special and favorite grandchildren: Nora and Zachary Noteman and Benjamin Levin.

Contents

Preface and Acknowledgments

T HE PRIVATE PRACTICE OF PSYCHOTHERAPY is physically and intellectually taxing, lonely, emotionally draining, sometimes financially uncertain, sometimes socially or professionally suspect. Often, however, it may be intellectually fascinating, emotionally rewarding, financially remunerative, and conducive to high social/professional status based on recognized service to individuals and the community. This book is written to help psychotherapists develop successful, lifelong careers in private practice within which the negatives listed above may be minimized and the positives maximized. It is intended to be of use to the psychotherapist contemplating entrance into private practice and to the more experienced professionals already so employed.

Hopefully, this book will be helpful, too, to clinic and agency staff, who may find some of the concepts, attitudes, and practices applicable and advantageous to their clients and themselves.

It is certainly my wish that academicians engaged in the education of clinicians include in the content of their courses something of what it's like to practice psychotherapy privately. They may be in the best position, as scholars, to articulate both the subtle and the substantial differences between agency-based practice and private practice. This book can serve as an important source for their purposes.

Most private practitioners of psychotherapy are psychiatrists, clinical psychologists, or clinical social workers, although increasing numbers of ministers, sociologists, psychiatric nurses, specialists in the treatment of alcoholism, geriatric specialists, sex therapists, family therapists, divorce counselors, death counselors, and others have recently undertaken this employment. My professional training, experience, and activity have been primarily in clinical social work. The basic theory informing my practice is psychoanalytic. The content of my writing, therefore, is dynamically oriented. Readers of differing theoretical persuasion or professional background are nevertheless likely to find this book helpful. Many studies of psychotherapy and psychotherapists have found that the concepts, attitudes, principles, and practices employed by psychotherapists of diverse professional backgrounds tend to look more and more alike the longer their years of experience.[1] That this should be so is not surprising. Psychotherapists are shaped by their clients at least as much as by their theory or training. Perhaps the core principles shared by all successful psychotherapists are the elusively simple ones of integrity and honesty, combined with an openness to hear, see, feel, and respond in a disciplined focused way.

When I entered private practice more than 20 years ago, I did so haltingly and somewhat apologetically. I feared financial failure and the possible disapproval of my colleagues. I feared that my motives would be viewed as venal. I acted as though I was making no decision and it was "just happening." In my heart of hearts, though, I wanted to be in private practice. The key attraction was the prospect of independence—of autonomy. I wanted the special pleasure of being an entrepreneur, "one who manages and assumes the risk of a business." Annie Dillard in her poetic, autobiographical book, *Pilgrim at Tinker Creek*, said: "The least brave act, chance taken and passage won, makes you feel loud as a child. But it gets harder." Looking back I wish I had acknowledged my decision more definitely at the time. I'd have enjoyed taking the chance more. It is a decision I have never regretted.

Let me tell you the circumstances. I was 35 years old, married, had three children, and lived in a southern suburb of Chicago. I was 10 years out of graduate school. For seven years I had been the executive director of a private, nonsectarian, suburban family service agency that had expanded under my leadership from one professional person to seven people, from one office to four locations. We were the first private family service agency in Illinois to initiate a state-funded mental health clinic as a division of our private agency. I felt successful, but restless to try something new. Perhaps I was experiencing the "seven-year itch," or I was at another adult developmental transition stage of the sort discussed by Levinson in *The Seasons of a Man's Life*.[2]

Throughout my career I had continued to be in direct practice, which I found more satisfying than administration. I had completed an intensive three-year training program in child care at the Chicago Institute for Psychoanalysis, had regularly participated in treatment seminars and consultations, read consistently, and generally "kept up" with treatment. Nevertheless, I felt it necessary to explore opportunities for better-paying, "challenging" administrative positions throughout the country. The more I investigated positions in psychiatric clinics, family and children's agencies, hospitals, and universities, the more discouraged I felt about investing the next important segment of my life in this way. In psychiatric clinics or hospitals I would forever be subordinate to physician control, in social agencies to board-of-directors control, in industry to other bureaucratic control. Yet the way to "success" in a career as a social worker, I was constantly reminded, lay through advancement in administration—or in academia. I knew of no men or women practitioners who had won wide respect through the choice of practice within an institution as a lifetime career. The few lifetime career practitioners I knew had "made it" in private practice.

The Saintly Entrepreneur

To be sure, most important life decisions are overdetermined: more is involved than the simple "realities" or conscious phenomena. I had undergone psychoanalysis early in my career. That experience helped me to understand the important identifications I had made early in my life with my parents' values and expectations. I had also come to understand some of the forces at work in me that inhibited certain aggressive, competitive strivings but permitted the expression of other kinds of ambitious undertakings. Briefly, and without being overly exhibitionistic, it was important to my mother for me to be successful financially. She had always admired her own father, who had been a successful entrepreneur. My father, on the other hand, also respected individuals who were successful financially but most admired those who were spiritually or philosophically oriented. He admired his own father for his simple, almost "saintlike" generosity and kindness. To please my father, therefore, it was important for me to be scholarly, humanitarian, and a servant of mankind—to be "saintly." To please my mother, it was important to be financially well-to-do and to possess status and power recognized by the community at large. Fortunately for me, I possessed certain talents and capacities including reasonable intelligence, ability to learn, and skill in articulating ideas, feelings, and abstract concepts. A number of choices were open to me initially in choosing a career, such as business and the professions of medicine, law, and the ministry. Any one of these might have provided the opportunity to express and make use of personal talents while meeting the parental demands that I had internalized. Certain "practical" life reasons, together with rebellious aspects of my personality, moved me in the direction of social work rather than to one of the other professions mentioned. Once I had chosen social work these internal forces propelled me in the direction of continuing direct treatment of individuals while simultaneously expressing entrepreneurial aspects of my personality. These were nicely combined in beginning a family service agency and helping it to grow while I continued to be in direct practice. Movement into private practice was an even more fulfilling choice. It provided the opportunity to increase my income and my status in the professional community as well as in the community at large, while simultaneously providing a humanitarian service of the most important and intimate kind to people in intense need and pain. I could be a "saintly entrepreneur"—although maturity makes me question the "saintliness."

In some ways, I permitted my patients to help me make the decision for private practice. I did this by announcing my resignation from my post as executive director and then permitted individuals who contacted me for consultation to see me privately. Colleagues within the professional community in and around Chicago helped make my decision by referring friends or relatives to me for direct service. I needed these external supports to assure me that I was not deviating too far from the professional norms of social work. I hoped that I was not behaving in too self-serving a way that would somehow displease my father's value demands.

The reader may need to be reminded that for social workers, the idea of charging fees for services was a relatively new one in the 1950s. Only a few agencies had begun to charge fees and usually these were nominal and not related to the actual cost of service. Ruth Fizdale had written a paper about fee charging,[3] and a few agencies had established special units where fees were charged. The orientation of social workers was to "service," and there seemed to be a contradiction between offering service and being paid for it. This sort of conflict was less important for psychiatrists or psychologists. Psychiatrists tend to think of their patients as conforming to a medical model of illness which the psychiatrist treats and is paid for in the conventional way any physician may be paid by his patient for treating illness. Perhaps as a consequence of my having been a patient in psychoanalysis, where I had paid a physician to treat me, my identification with him helped me to enter private practice.

During the past 20 years, of course, fee charging by mental health clinics, public agencies, and social service agencies has become more the norm, and more and more practitioners have entered into private practice. The kinds of conflicts that I experienced more than 20 years ago are no longer as likely to burden young psychotherapists contemplating private practice now. Nevertheless, there are certain conflicts that are likely to persist. For example, one deterrent from entering private practice was the recognition that I would have to give up certain power and status gratifications as the director of an important community agency. I would also give up the close daily social and professional contact with colleagues and members of the community. As all of us know, separation is painful and human beings often make great sacrifices to avoid it. Choosing a career in private practice of psychotherapy generally requires this kind of separation.

Separation Stress

Like many others before me and since, I chose to ease the pain of separation by moving into private practice on a part-

time basis while maintaining other kinds of professional contacts and employment. I became a consultant to agencies; I took
on responsibilities with the public school system for teaching
"sex education"; I took a position as a researcher in a study of
aid to dependent children; and I solicited speaking engage-
ments on family life and child care for lay people. Each of these
was part-time, put me in touch with many professional and
community people, helped sustain me financially, and, as it
turned out, helped to build my private practice.

Acknowledgments

Before closing this preface, I must offer thanks to several
people who have been most helpful in this book's creation.
First, my wife Elaine has suffered patiently with me while
simultaneously encouraging and pressing me forward. My long-
time associate, colleague, and dear friend Frank Barnett has
offered support, advice, and deeply rich help beyond measure.
To Estelle Gabriel, who has served as a role model par excel-
lence, I owe great gratitude. Professor Arthur Schwartz of the
University of Chicago first urged me to write this book and introduced me to Gladys Topkis, then of The Free Press, who had
the confidence in me to ask me to proceed. Joyce Seltzer of The
Free Press has offered invaluable editorial assistance in
straightening out muddled construction and organization. Terri
Morandi, my secretary, waded through my hen-print scribbling
and brought order out of chaos. And my gratitude goes out to
literally thousands of clients and colleagues who taught me almost everything that is included here.

A.M.L., Chicago, Illinois, January 1983

CHAPTER 1

On Choosing
Private Practice

"The least brave act, chance taken and passage won, makes you feel loud as a child. But it gets harder."

Annie Dillard, from *Pilgrim at Tinker Creek*

T HE PURPOSE OF MY DESCRIPTION of my entrance into private practice was not to suggest it as a model, but to identify some of the issues anyone may face in career planning or changing. The actual process of planning one's career is a continuous and changing one. At different stages of one's life, career planning takes on different coloration. As with any kind of planning, one needs to differentiate between *goals* and *objectives*. Goals tend to be long-range, while objectives tend to be relatively short-range, aimed at the achievement of the goals. For example, at age 25 one might have the *goal* that by age 35 he will be in full-time private practice. His immediate *objectives* might be to acquire the competence and reputation to move toward that goal and to explore the opportunities for achieving it.

At age 25 one is likely to be employed in a clinic, hospital, or agency full-time as a psychologist, psychiatrist, or clinical social worker. The acquisition of competence is a never-ending process, but learning tends to be greater and faster when one is younger. At least partly, the pressure of having to deal with

new situations fosters learning. Careful selection of a work site
that provides rich learning opportunities is important in order
to accomplish the immediate objective of gaining competence
and the confidence that accompanies it. Most young practitioners must seek out or make opportunities to gain recognition
among colleagues and within the broader community. As he
considers the long-range goal of being in private practice, each
practitioner needs to ask himself a number of important questions. Some of these are: "What do I do well? What do I do
poorly? What do I tend to spend most time on voluntarily?
What activities do I shun? What activity gives me a sense of
satisfaction? What gives me very little satisfaction?"

The answers to these questions will spring from one's unconscious as well as from conscious intellectual processes.
Many of those who enter social work, for example, are interested in bringing about major social, economic, and political
changes. In the course of graduate social work training some
come to the conclusion that work with individuals to change
their own immediate life situations is more interesting and feasible. Others are satisfied by the work of attempting to bring
about more global changes and are less satisfied working with
troubled individuals. For those who contemplate the private
practice of psychotherapy, work with individuals to try to bring
about change in their lives or in their family relationships must
hold primary interest.

Autonomy

The biggest and most important question that must be considered by anyone contemplating private practice is, "How
much do I enjoy working autonomously?" The truth is that to
work autonomously is a burden. To be sure, there are compen-
sating gratifications. But many, perhaps most, professionals by

virtue of their individual life histories and psychological make-up find that autonomous functioning is too burdensome, and they prefer to work as a member of a team where decisions and direction are shared. Whatever the model of private practice, however, autonomous practice is the sine qua non.

Other aspects of private practice will be either satisfying or dissatisfying, depending on conscious and unconscious wishes, needs, and desires. There are some of us who find the role of entrepreneur to be distasteful, while others relish it. Some of us need to gratify our own need to be "givers" and not detract from this gratification by having a fee-for-service arrangement with a patient. Others feel a greater sense of self-appreciation by virtue of having the patient pay for time. The patient confirms that we are offering something of value to him. Another major consideration for many of us is that of personal or professional identity and/or image.

Clinical social workers probably have a more difficult time than either psychologists or psychiatrists in relation to public image and professional identity. The professional image of social workers tends to be blurred and confused. The public generally is unaware of their professional training and skill especially in psychotherapy. Their clients will often refer to them as "psychologists" or call them "doctor" despite clear avowals that they are "clinical social workers." They have little "brand name" recognition. For many social workers, professional identity is derived from association or affiliation with a well-recognized institution like a major training hospital or social agency. Psychiatrists and psychologists, too, derive a certain professional status through affiliation with respected institutions, but they derive even more from their respective profession qua profession. Their public credibility is enhanced, and their personal feelings of professional identity are strengthened. The isolation of full-time private practice may detract from one's sense of professional identity and deter many from such practice. For some people it is possible to have a full-time private practice and maintain affiliation with a major institution, thereby solving the problem. But for many this is not possible. It would be foolhardy for anyone to enter into private practice if professional identity is of high importance and in any way appears to be threatened by giving up institutional affiliations.

Entry into private practice may occur at almost any time during a career, just like exit from private practice may take place at any time. Indeed, there is reason to believe that people move about from position to position experimentally throughout their working lives until they find the most acceptable niche for them. Trade-offs are made in almost every aspect of life throughout its course, and nowhere is this more evident than in the work place. Studies of work satisfaction indicate that older workers are more satisfied by their work than younger workers, perhaps as a result of this movement from position to position.[4]

Women in Private Practice

During the early 1970s a survey of more than 600 mid-career, middle-aged graduates of the School of Social Service Administration at the University of Chicago who had been out of school 25 years or more was completed (Levin, 1976).[5] A solid majority were satisfied with their careers, and few would change any of the major decisions they had made along the way. Whether they were academicians, administrators, or clinicians, they seemed to be satisfied with their jobs. This finding was not unlike those in other studies of job satisfaction where the older the worker, the more satisfied he was with his job. Nevertheless, in this study academicians were the most satisfied and clinicians the least. Most of the clinicians were married women employed in institutions rather than in private practice; many of them had interrupted their careers to raise families. The key issue accounting for the difference in degree of satisfaction appeared to be the degree of autonomy attainable rather than the substance of their work, status, or income.

All in all, these findings may be reassuring to young professionals charting their future careers. They can be reasonably optimistic that whatever career line they choose, it will bring reasonable satisfaction. However, there were other disturbing aspects of the study—especially as they relate to women. Many wrote addenda to the survey indicating what many modern feminists and others have observed: that women setting out in the 1940s and 1950s had far fewer "acceptable" career options open to them. Furthermore, women found the "nurturing" aspects of clinical practice more "acceptable" for them than did the men. It is not stretching too far to speculate that sexism played an important part in assigning less status and autonomy to the practitioner-clinician role within employing social institutions. Private practice may lead women out of this second-class status situation. And private practice may also provide a career line for men that is less "tainted" by sexist views.

Men or women who change careers in their forties, fifties, or older are, of course, no longer a novelty. For women who interrupt careers to raise families, private practice is a viable alternative. For men who want to expand their professional lives from administrative or academic life, it may be an interesting opportunity.

Mid-Career Changes

Recently, a psychologist in his fifties described his move from his position as administrator of a university mental health clinic into full-time private practice. He became aware that if he were to continue to advance as an administrator, he would have to give up patient contact. This prospect pushed him into a reappraisal of what he wanted most, and private practice was his choice. As he talked about his choice, he sounded very much like the people described by Levinson (1978) in *The Seasons of a Man's Life*. Levinson wrote that men going through the transition from early into middle adulthood often ask:

> What have I done with my life? What do I really get from and give to my wife, children, friends, work, community—and self? What is it I truly want? What are my real values? What are my greatest talents and how am I using or wasting them? What have I done with my early dream? Can I live in a way that best combines my current desires, values, talents and aspirations?[6]

For this psychologist, it had become tiresome to continue battling with his administration over budgetary, staffing, salary, and other bureaucratic necessities. He no longer derived much satisfaction from the status and power associated with successful progress in the bureaucratic hierarchy. He enjoyed that aspect of administration that permitted him to function as "mentor" to younger staff, but even that opportunity seemed decreasingly possible. And like the middle-aged people studied by Neugarten (1968), he felt a greater sense of self-awareness, selectivity, mastery, and competence as a person than he had felt when he was younger. He felt no longer "driven" but more the "driver," more "in command."[7]

His opting for private practice permitted him to spend more of his time doing what he liked to do best. He gained more leisure time and more discretionary time to devote to his family and community interests.

Women who have interrupted or postponed their careers to raise children may go through their mid-life transition in a comparable but somewhat different manner. They may ask the same questions as middle-aged men, but in order effectively to resume a career or to embark upon a new one, they may need to make necessary arrangements for family and work, may need to secure further training, and may need to work out a career plan. Perhaps the most important aspect of preparation required for mid-life women is the acquisition once again of a sense of professional competence and confidence. They may have that sense in relation to most aspects of their lives but may need special preparation to reattain it professionally and to plan their careers after long interruption. However, as Neugarten notes, "Despite the new realization of the finiteness of time, one of the most prevailing themes expressed by these middle-aged respondents is that middle adulthood is a period of maximum capacities and ability to handle a highly complex environment and a highly differentiated self."[8] These attributes are most useful for the private practice of psychotherapy.

The Three Main Professional Groups: Psychiatrists, Clinical Psychologists, Clinical Social Workers

The three main professional groups who make psychotherapy their occupation—clinical psychiatrists, clinical psychologists, and clinical social workers—probably enter their respective professions for somewhat differing reasons. Clinical psychiatrists enter medicine to become physicians and cure illness, ultimately specializing in mental illness. Clinical psychologists tend to be interested early in the science of the workings of the mind and of human behavior. Clinical social workers tend to want to help the poor, the downtrodden, and the less fortunate, often by bringing about social change or by other "problem-solving" efforts.

Historically, medicine, including psychiatry, began and developed as a solo or partnership profession, while social work began as an organizational practice and psychology as an academic enterprise. Schools of social work oriented their students to become employees of agencies; departments of psychology oriented their students for an academic life; and medical schools tended to point their young doctors toward private practice.

A consequence of these differences among the professions is a differing attitude toward private practice. Clinical social workers and clinical psychologists entering private practice have tended to feel like deviants and have suffered feelings of uncertainty and even of illegitimacy. To be sure, the increasing number of clinical social workers and clinical psychologists entering private practice during the past 25 years has eased this tension, but they still represent relatively small minorities of their professions. Clinical psychiatrists have an easier time of it, but they may suffer from another problem: that their physician colleagues and others question their authenticity as physicians so that to some extent they too feel like deviants.

Henry (1971),[9] who coined the term "Psychotherapy: the fifth profession," (after medicine, law, theology, and news reporting), pointed out that because of similarities in outlook, goals, education, skill, and competencies, clinical social workers, clinical psychologists, and clinical psychiatrists might well merge into a new profession called "Psychotherapy." Up to now, however, the professions have not merged into a single professional community that has developed a common control structure. Therefore, psychotherapy is and will continue to be practiced in the foreseeable future by members of the several separate professions. Each of these professions must provide the control structure, and members must continue to abide by their controls in order to practice as professionals. Fortunately, while there are differences between the professions, there is great similarity between their codes of ethics and other control structures, and the internal differences among members of the respective professions are likely to be greater than the between-group differences.

Another of the things that the three professions are likely to have in common is an absence in their training of education about what it's like to set up and manage a private practice.

This book is designed to be helpful to all psychotherapists, whatever their specific professional identity and background, in filling that gap.

Conventions Employed in This Book

Several conventions are used throughout the book for convenience. Psychotherapists are referred to as "he," which is meant to include both women and men. Consumers of psychotherapy are referred to as "patients" and "clients" interchangeably. This reflects the definition of psychotherapy used in this book, which is a practice where the healing influence is mainly achieved through verbal communications, acts, or rituals, and where the receiver of psychotherapy is not necessarily defined as mentally sick.

CHAPTER 2

What Is the Private Practice of Psychotherapy?

The physician as a small businessman and independent entrepreneur will share the fate of the dodo and the dinosaur: extinction.''

Harry Schwartz, in the *Wall Street Journal*, 1981

It IS SAID that once when Freud was asked to define briefly what constituted "mental health," he responded, "To work and to love." Most of us would agree that feelings of independence, freedom, and security are pleasurable. They are connected with our ability to guarantee our own existence by our own achievements, that is, through our work. The practice of psychotherapy is, of course, work.

Through the course of history work elaborated beyond economic necessity and evolved into specialized forms, occupations, vocations, and professions. Many would say that the chief goal of professionals as differentiated from other occupations or businesses is to provide professional services to a client. Profit making must be the by-product. Professions are thought to possess two unique characteristics: (1) an ethic in which professional decisions are not predicated on self-interest, and (2) a control structure lodged in the professional community.

The definition of private practice adopted by social workers probably is readily applicable to all the professions practicing psychotherapy. It states, "A private practitioner is a social worker, who wholly or in part, practices his profession outside a governmental or duly incorporated voluntary agency, who has responsibility for his own practice and sets up his own conditions of exchange with his clients. . . ."[10]

In the private practice of psychotherapy the essence of professionalism and professional controls are of paramount importance, since the controls of bureaucratic employing organizations are absent. In bureaucracies, performance is controlled by the directives received from superiors rather than by self-imposed standards and peer-group surveillance, as is the case among professionals in private practice. Bureaucracy competes with the professional community for control of the practitioner. Bureaucratic control puts the employer in a powerful position to entice the professional to yield to the organization his autonomy and loyalty to his profession and its principles. While private practice provides the opportunity to maintain first loyalty to the profession and to patients, it is a business or entrepreneurial venture. Therefore, conflict may exist between the goal of serving clients' interests and the goal of profit making. This conflict may create stress within the practitioner.

The popular conception of the true profession has focused upon the free and autonomous nature of professional occupations. Yet today most professionals are salaried employees of bureaucratic organizations. The free autonomous professional is the exception. Indeed, the trend among all professions is toward collectivization. Nevertheless, some professional psychotherapists continue to find greater satisfaction in private practice than in institutions. Satisfaction or dissatisfaction with a career seems to be most heavily influenced by the following factors: (1) the conditions (or context) of the work, (2) the nature of the task and the ability to perform it (or its substance), (3) personal status and income in a bureaucratic hierarchy or position in a professional hierarchy, (4) status of the profession in the larger society, and (5) some sense of move-ment and/or accomplishment on a time-life line. Let's see how these factors look in choosing the private practice of psycho-therapy as a career as contrasted with other career lines.

The outstanding differences between private practice and organizational practice of psychotherapy are that there are within any bureaucracy greater constraints on autonomy and a greater lack of community recognition of professional author-ity. For example, in the private setting one chooses the location, size, furnishings, and equipment of one's own office within the parameters of self-set budget and taste. Private practitioners determine their own hourly, daily, weekly, annual work sched-ules in accordance with their own idiosyncratic preferences. They choose the kinds of clients, types of problems, methodolo-gies to be employed, length of treatment sessions, fees, dura-tion of treatment, and termination. All the conditions of treat-ment are set between practitioner and patient rather than determined by an organizational directive.

On the other hand, there is much greater opportunity for informal consultation and peer socializing in clinics or agen-cies. Social contacts in the work place are an important factor in satisfaction or dissatisfaction. Usually, even in private group practices, opportunities for them are drastically limited be-cause of time pressures. In addition, salary income may be much more dependable, and there may be much less time and energy invested in mundane bookkeeping matters. However, in-stitutional record-keeping requirements are far more time-con-suming than those in private practice.

Psychotherapy conducted within institutions theoretically should differ little from that conducted in private practice. Un-fortunately, there are many institutional forces that belie this assumption.

First of all, clients of private practitioners tend to be mid-dle- or upper-class, while those of agency practitioners tend to be people of lower socioeconomic status. In a recent study,

Borenzweig (1981) found that agency practitioners saw more people whom they labeled as psychotic than did respondents in private practice; most of the clients seen in private practice were diagnosed as psychoneurotic.[11]

There is some likelihood that clients who are disturbing to their families or society will appear with greater frequency in agencies, while those who are disturbed within themselves will appear with greater frequency in private practice. Borenzweig found, for example, that private practitioners appeared to be less likely than agency practitioners to have children as clients. Conversely, private practitioners were more likely to treat young adults. Perhaps the "YAVIS" principle is illustrated here. "YAVIS" is the acronym for "Young, Attractive, Verbal, Intelligent, and Sexy"—the kind of client with whom almost every therapist prefers to work because prognosis and progress are generally more hopeful.

Since one of the most important elements of work satisfaction is the nature of the task and the ability to perform it successfully, it is easy to believe that the private practitioner has the better of it on this score. Furthermore, private practitioners tend to spend more work time in direct service to clients, where they may attain a greater sense of accomplishment, than do psychotherapists in institutions, where more time must be invested in committee and other nondirect service work.

Another of Borenzweig's findings that is of special interest is that private practitioners tend to use psychoanalytic techniques and one-to-one treatment modalities, while agency practitioners tend to use art therapy, "homework assignments," chemotherapy, and psychological testing more frequently. Borenzweig expressed "surprise" to discover that agency practitioners use what he calls "more innovative modalities."[12] Many experienced psychotherapists, however, would argue that often so-called "innovative modalities" are the psychotherapeutic counterpart of "fast food" service—cheaper and quicker but less satisfying and less nourishing. Indeed, many agency practitioners experience a sense of frustration in their practice as a result of feeling administrative pressure to be "quick" in treatment, foreclosing the opportunity to experience the satisfaction of doing "good work" with their patients over a longer time span or with more intensive contacts.

Private Practice as a Career

The road to "success" in bureaucratic settings is to leave direct practice with patients and move into supervision, administration, or academia. There is no "career ladder" to traverse in direct clinical practice in most agencies or clinics. This holds true for clinical psychologists, psychiatrists, and clinical social workers. Rewards are controlled and distributed by the bureaucracy rather than by the professions.[13]

Private practice is a way to create and move up a career ladder. Indeed, within the hierarchies of the professions, the private practitioner is likely to win status as high as or even higher than that of most administrators by virtue of his greater income and autonomy, attributes that tend to be admired in most societies. If, in addition, he publishes and/or teaches, he may very well attain even greater respect and status than many outstanding academicians who are not actively engaged in practice. On the other hand, more and more of the better-respected clinically oriented academicians combine practice with teaching and research, and they perhaps most of all have tended to make private practice more respectable and accepted among all the psychotherapeutic professions.

While all the professions included under the umbrella of psychotherapy attain a substantial part of their status from their individual professional affiliations, a considerable part of it is the status accorded to the practice of psychotherapy itself by the larger society. Professional status in a highly competitive society tends to be associated with a wide number of variables, not all of which appear to be very sensible. The most important of these appear to be the length of time spent in training and experience required to practice the profession, the degree of difficulty or mastery the problems dealt with are perceived to entail, the extent of the power of the professional, the degree to which the professional is autonomous, and the potential level of income attainable. Fortunately for many professionals, like neurosurgeons, oncologists, and, perhaps, psychotherapists, status is not directly related to the degree of success in the outcomes of their interventions. "The operation was a success, but the patient died," is all too frequently the case among many of the highest-status professions.

Psychotherapists, particularly in private practice, appear to be accorded relatively high status publicly, despite a concurrent tendency to disparage psychotherapy itself. Perhaps the degree to which emotional problems and their treatment are viewed as mystifying leads to some feeling of awe toward those engaged with them. Whatever the determinants, rational or irrational, psychotherapists gain a certain degree of career/ work satisfaction from this attributed status, especially when they are visible as independent professionals in private practice rather than being another "employee" of an agency or clinic.

Perhaps the most important source of satisfaction for the practitioner who makes a lifetime career in psychotherapy is the cumulative recognition of clients helped over a lifetime, the increasing respect accorded him by colleagues and the public, and by his own awareness of increasing perceptiveness regarding the problems presented.

Women and Private Practice

The driving force central to all approaches to psychotherapy appears to be the power of the relationship between the therapist and the client. "Nurturing," "care-giving," "re-parenting," and "affirmation of worth" are fundaments upon which the relationship is built. Probably because of underlying sexist attitudes in our Western culture, nurturing, giving, and parenting (mothering) are often seen as "feminine attributes" and consequently "weaker" and less valuable, while scientific carefully methodical behaviors are viewed as "masculine" and consequently "stronger" and more valuable. These views have probably influenced career choices of men and women in regard to the three major professions practicing psychotherapy—at least until recently. In a survey of social workers in mid-life referred to earlier, a frequent comment by women respondents was that they chose social work as a career at least partly because it was one of the few options acceptably open to them as women in the 1940s and 1950s.[14] Nowadays, fortunately, more and more women are entering psychiatry, psychology, and other professions though, unfortunately, no similar trend seems evident in the flow of men into social work. Perhaps the entry of women into all of the professions may tend to move them all in the direction of accepting "feminine" approaches less self-consciously or apologetically. And perhaps the movement of women into private practice may lead to a changing view of "hard-nose," "masculine" entrepreneurial activities as more acceptably "feminine." It may contribute to breaking down artificial misconceptions of both psychotherapy and private practice and may further humanize both.

Despite the great advances that have been made during the past decade in expanding equal career opportunities for women, it appears that women still assume (or have thrust upon them) the primary responsibility for child care. Private practice provides a career opportunity for women who wish to or are constrained to combine child and family care with a satisfying career. It provides the chance to arrange time more flexibly and at their own discretion. There is alarming statistical evidence that increasing numbers of women are and will be raising children as single parents; private practice stands as an especially attractive career option for them. For those men and women who have moved to new levels of assumption of equal responsibility for child care, private practice provides an attractive option for men to structure their careers in a way that enables them too to be available to their children and their mates flexibly.

Nevertheless, it must be said that the private practice of psychotherapy is demanding, not easy work. Therapists pour out great energy in nurturing and caring for their patients. Successful, satisfying family relationships are themselves, despite the investment demanded to make them work, probably the best antidote to professional "burn-out." Indeed, one of the greatest vulnerabilities to which psychotherapists are exposed is the tendency to turn to patients for the intimate personal/emotional gratifications so essential to us all when these are lacking in the therapists' personal lives.

The Nature of Psychotherapy

It may be appropriate at this point to discuss what psychotherapy is wherever and by whomever it is practiced. Obviously, the field is complicated, branching out in hundreds of biomedical, behavioral, psychoanalytic, individual, family, group, and other directions. At least 250 different therapies have been identified as in use today. Approximately 29,000 psychiatrists, 26,000 clinical psychologists, 31,000 mental health social workers, 10,000 psychiatric nurses, 10,000 counselors, and untold numbers of unlicensed people offer their services to the public privately or within public institutions, according to Dava Sobel.[15] As one psychiatrist put it in the same article, "Unfortunately, choosing a therapist is like choosing a restaurant. If you go to a Chinese restaurant, you get Chinese food. With us, if you see an analyst, you'll be on the couch. If you walk into a psychopharmacologist's office, you'll walk out with a prescription. If you go to a behaviorist, you'll probably be taught relaxation techniques and biofeedback."[16] Nevertheless, all the more prominent theoretical schools of thought accept the notion that successful therapy is based on a more or less close human relationship between therapist and patient. Psychiatrists may tend to think of emotional disturbance as "illness" and of their interventions as "curative." Psychologists may tend to think in a similar way but with an orientation toward a developmental or "learning" model to explain pathology, and might use a more "cognitive" approach in their efforts to bring about amelioration or change. Clinical social workers may tend to regard disturbances as socially determined and to use their relationship with the client as the base upon which to build change, growth, and problem-solving skills. The driving force common to all three, however, is the power of the relationship.

Since the focus of this book is on private practice rather than on an exposition of psychotherapy, further discussion may best be reserved for another time and place. It may be concluded from this chapter that the private practice of psychotherapy is work, carried out within the parameters of professional codes of ethics and generally accepted modes of practice, by professionals of varying backgrounds and training, with widely divergent kinds of clients. Lifelong careers in private practice may be demanding yet rewarding.

In the next chapter the challenge of private practice and assessing one's readiness to engage in it are discussed.

CHAPTER 3

Readiness for Private Practice: Competence, Commitment, and Credibility

"Who would want surgery from a physician who is nervous, does not like surgery, is insecure about what to charge and wonders where his next case is coming from?"

Marquis Wallace, unpublished doctoral dissertation

R̲EADINESS FOR PRIVATE PRACTICE must be defined by each individual practitioner within the context of existing state and local laws and the requirements of his respective profession.
Training, experience, licensing, and/or professional accreditation are obvious considerations. But personal/emotional commitment and credibility are at least as important. These latter
are likely to be expressed attitudinally and behaviorally by the
therapist through an obvious liking for and comfort with his
work.

Education and Personal Psychotherapy

Training or education for psychotherapy varies significantly both within each of the professions and between them.
Most of the therapists Henry (1971)[17] surveyed, including psychiatrists, clinical social workers, and psychologists, credited

27

their academic training less than their own personal therapy with being helpful to their learning how to practice psychotherapy. Freud (1980)[18] was the first to assert that medical knowledge contributes nothing, literally nothing, to the understanding and treatment of neurotic personalities. And Raimy (1950)[19] waggishly commented that psychotherapy is "an unidentified technique applied to unspecified problems with unpredictable outcomes. For this technique we recommend vigorous-training."

The question of personal therapy as a requirement for the training process is itself unresolved, except for psychoanalytic training. Most psychotherapists, whatever their profession or theoretical persuasion, would, however, probably agree that some experience with personal therapy is invaluable if not an absolute necessity. Surgeons seem to derive a greater appreciation of what it's like to be operated on after they've experienced surgery themselves. Personal psychotherapy for psychotherapists may be even more essential, not just to experience "what it's like," but to expand and deepen the therapist's experience of himself, his conflicts, vulnerabilities, predilections, self-constructed myths, prejudices, and strengths. There are many who would argue that in order to listen to and hear others, one must feel that he himself has been listened to and heard well. Further, the quintessence of psychotherapeutic efforts appears more and more to be the therapist's ability to relate empathically to his patient. Personal psychotherapy tends to increase the therapist's empathic readiness by reducing his internal pain or stress so that he may attend to his patient. An obvious though simplistic example is that of a therapist suffering a toothache. His ability to attend to his patient is likely to be significantly impaired until his own pain is moderated. Psychic pain may be even more distracting, particularly if it is disguised or coped with automatically and without the conscious awareness that may be derived from psychotherapy.

In addition, personal psychotherapy or psychoanalysis may be treated as a deductible business expense. A clinical social worker in private practice as a co-therapist with a psychiatrist undertook psychotherapy primarily to improve her skills as a social worker, but also to alleviate general anxiety and depression. In a recent ruling, the Tax Court concluded that she was entitled to a business deduction for education expenses under Section 1.162-5(a)(1) of the Income Tax Regulations. The court said that personal analysis for clinical social workers is widely accepted and commonplace. Under the Regulations, the court said, "education need not be restricted to formal instruction and, as at psychoanalytic institutes, can include a student's personal analysis.[20]

The court also concluded that the education did in fact improve the taxpayer's skills in her present employment. "A deeper self-understanding . . . contributes directly to an improvement in a therapist's diagnostic skills; a clinical social worker must be able to separate her personal problems from those of her patients so that she can properly diagnose and treat them," said the court.

Curricula and experiential or apprenticeship requirements vary widely, and are heavily influenced by the theoretical or ideological orientation of the particular institution that offers training. Individual supervisors differ dramatically in their outlook. Within each of the professions there has generally been stressful conflict between the academicians and those who want to "just learn how to be a good clinician."

Frank (1975)[21] has asserted that features of the therapist's personality and style that counteract his patient's sense of being demoralized are more important determinants of his success than are his specific procedures. He cites warmth, genuineness, and empathy as the vital attributes of a successful therapist. He recommends that therapists familiarize themselves with a wide variety of approaches and master those that best fit their different patients. An underemphasized function of the therapist's having some kind of conceptual schema to guide his efforts, according to Frank, is to sustain his interest in the patient and to reassure him of the validity of his efforts in the face of therapeutic failures. "It ain't so much *what* you do but *how* you do it" seems to be the message.

Where to Find Appropriate Training and Experience

Many long-experienced therapists would probably be in general agreement with Frank's observations. Extrapolating from these in regard to choosing the best place to get training and experience for psychotherapy suggests that institutions where there are a wide variety of patients, theoretical and ideological ideas, and methodologies present are the most desirable. Young therapists with limited clinical experience may need to strike a balance between a smorgasbord of theories and methodologies and a too narrowly rigid adherence to a single school of thought. Arriving at a theoretical, methodological, and ideological stance with which one is comfortable becomes a building block for feelings of competence and confidence which are essential for genuine commitment.

In recent years, new institutions have developed that offer training in psychotherapy at the graduate or postgraduate level. Institutes for psychoanalysis are probably the best known. Generally they are open only to physicians, although a growing number are open to other professions. Some of them offer special courses to nonmedical people, especially in child therapy to clinical social workers. Students with an undergraduate degree may enroll in one of several schools of professional psychology, which generally offer a four-year full-time program culminating in the award of a Psy.D. (doctor of psychology) degree. These programs emphasize clinical practice rather than research, which is the usual emphasis in academic psychology. Institutes for clinical social work have also come into existence recently, accepting students who already hold a master's degree in social work. These emphasize clinical practice and may award a Ph.D. or a DCSW (doctor of clinical social work) degree. Opportunities for formal training in psychotherapy are expanding, but usually outside traditional and academic settings. New York, Washington, D.C., Los Angeles, and Chicago tend to have the largest number of programs available; new ones are opening up elsewhere.

Licensing and Accreditation by Profession

Licensing of psychotherapists is a muddy, politically driven mess, and is often the field upon which "turf" issues between the several professions are played out. The central question in licensing of psychotherapists is: Is psychotherapy a part of medicine and, therefore, to be practiced only by physicians? Licensing of professions tends to be reserved to the states, and laws vary widely. All the states have laws regulating medical practice, and many, but not all, of these refer to the treatment of mental and nervous disorders as part of medicine. Psychologists are regulated in some way in all the states, and social workers are regulated in 21 states. A few states have laws regulating marriage and family counselors, pastoral counselors, "social psychotherapists," hypnotherapists, and others. Licensing is, of course, closely related to third-party payment. Specific information regarding requirements that psychotherapists must meet in each state may be obtained from each state's regulatory body. It should be noted that in some states a psychotherapist may practice within a public agency without holding a license, but must have one if he engages in private practice. Further, some municipalities require special licensing locally, and these requirements should be checked out. For a deeper look into issues of licensing for psychotherapists, the reader is directed to Hogan (1979).[22]

Each of the several professions has independent accrediting procedures. Psychiatry has a set of requirements including an approved residency and an examination to win "Board certification" in psychiatry and neurology. Psychology has a National Registry listing which requires an approved doctorate including a clinical practicum. And social work has two National Registries each of which requires similar education and experience. Both require that the experience be in direct supervised clinical work, and that the graduate education must be in the clinical area. (The reason for two registries is related to political differences within the social work profession. One is sponsored by the National Association of Social Workers, and the other by the National Federation of Societies of Clinical Social Work.)

Above and beyond these basic requirements of the professions, most would recommend additional experience before embarking on independent private practice. Experience working intensively with disturbed patients with extensive supervision and consultation and increasing autonomous practice is advisable.

Commitment

Beyond consideration of specified norms of the several professions for independent practice, it is important for anyone contemplating private practice to think about the issue of commitment to private practice in a way that draws a parallel to commitment to any entrepreneurial enterprise.

Entrepreneurs must be prepared to take risks. The private practitioner must be prepared to risk money—or loss of income—and loss of a social/professional base that has been emotionally sustaining. In many ways, the private practitioner is like the small businessman in the community, while the administrators of hospitals, clinics, and agencies tend to act and to think in terms similar to those of the managers of corporations and conglomerates. The fundamental difference between administrators and psychotherapists in private practice is that administrators focus on control of their staff and organization, while the practitioners focus on helping their clients gain mastery over themselves and their environments and strive to accomplish this within an environment which leaves them as free as possible. The path to success for the administrator is to manage and control larger and larger enterprises. The path to success for the therapist-entrepreneur leads to the "bottom line" of profit, but he is likely to be more interested in going his own way. In that respect, the psychotherapist as entrepreneur is somewhat of an anomaly—neither corporate manager nor aggressive individual entrepreneur anxious to build an ever-expanding business. Perhaps the private practitioner is most like the skilled individual craftsman of earlier times—a type sorely missed and much sought after in our time. He plies his trade on his own, learning as much as he can along the way. Perhaps private practitioners are an anomalous group in this day of corporate enterprise in so many areas of life—science, education medicine, and industry. Maybe they will not survive, will become extinct like the dodo, as Schwartz predicts. But to increase their chances of survival, they need to exercise some of the best entrepreneurial skills, fed by scientific research and treatment experience.

Andrew Hacker[23] finds "the shame of professional schools" to be "that the schools care surprisingly little about the needs of their own students, or those of the larger society our professions supposedly serve." He discusses schools of law, business, and medicine, but for our purposes his comments about medical training are most relevant. While acknowledging the great scientific medical achievements of our time, he says:

> At the same time, the lofty level of medical education has left a gaping hole in the national health care. Seldom do medical professors, all of whom are specialists, offer students simple hints on how to help someone who comes to a doctor's office with a

vague complaint. Yet, that is where medical practice should begin and where medicine is still an art. It demands a temperament that takes individuals seriously, joined with an intuition for sensing what is wrong. Perhaps those qualities can't be taught. If not, medical schools would do well to give greater preferences to applicants who seem to have them. He goes on to say that "we are turning out professionals who tend to look on people as something of a bother. Not surprisingly, more than a few patients, clients, and customers are beginning to rebel. . . . With an oversupply of professionals, some may forget what they were taught in school and begin to ask how they might be of service."

Psychotherapists in private practice must represent the antithesis to the negative stereotype described. To be sure, they are in practice to earn their livelihood as entrepreneurs. But simultaneously their livelihoods are based on their willingness and skillful ability to serve those who seek them out. The private practitioner must make a dual commitment to independent, autonomous entrepreneurship and to psychotherapy that serves the patient best within the context of his need.

Webster's defines commitment as "(a) A promise or pledge to do something . . . , (b) An open declaration of adherence, as to a scientific hypothesis."[24] Commitment to the private practice of psychotherapy must be made in two parts: (1) to the practice of psychotherapy, and (2) specifically to private practice. The practitioner's commitment is first to himself, second to his profession, and third to the consumer public. Naturally, as with all human decisions and activities, commitments are overdetermined and often are arrived at in a somewhat haphazard rather than orderly fashion. Nevertheless, it may be helpful to anyone contemplating private practice to consider his decision in relation to each of these several dimensions. Many professionals including lawyers, dentists, doctors, and others, in addition to psychotherapists, have wavered in commitment both to their particular profession and to private practice. Some of them are not so fortunate, and their ambivalence costs them dearly.

Commitment to the practice of psychotherapy probably must come first. Each of the several professions offers options to its members. Psychiatrists may, for example, enter into psychopharmacology or the other "medical" treatments, such as shock treatment or hospital-based treatment where direct patient-therapist interaction may be minimized, with direct intervention left to nurses, social work aides, and others, or they may enter into forensic psychiatry and other kinds of practice. Psychologists may limit themselves to doing diagnostic evaluations, forensic psychology, or other limited "counseling" that is short of psychotherapy, or may turn to industrial counseling to organizations or personnel-management counseling as distinguished from psychotherapy. Social workers may turn to administering programs or agencies, short-term contacts with children or adults, as in adoption, foster placement evaluations, or child custody evaluations. Marriage and family counselors and pastoral counselors may choose to stay away from psychotherapy, and limit themselves to teaching or preaching about family life.

A commitment to practice psychotherapy usually implies a willingness to work one-to-one, or with families or other small groups of people who are suffering from some kind of emotional distress. The commitment to psychotherapy usually means a willingness to work with the people in relation to their needs for as long a period of time as is required to bring about relief. There is obviously a broad variation of commitment of time and energy as between psychoanalytic therapy, which may be expected to continue from three to ten or more years with high frequency of contacts, and the brief therapies like "task-centered treatment" where "contracts" are for much more time-limited and goal-limited work. Despite the variations, the psychotherapist who intends to practice privately and therefore expects to develop an ongoing practice must expect to be in a community and available to his patients for an extended period.

Long-Range Time Commitment and Continuity

One of the dimensions of commitment less immediately visible in deciding to practice psychotherapy privately is that of time. By way of illustration, an interesting phenomenon was described recently by a colleague. A patient whom he had seen for a relatively brief series of sessions which were terminated in a way both agreed was successful returned almost 15 years later (at age 80). She reported the comfort she had experienced over the years from the knowledge she had "that you were still there in your office—just in case." What shall this be called— an unresolved "positive transference," a "placebo" effect? Or shall we say the therapist rendered a community mental health service—perhaps more powerful than valium? No matter, except that in relation to building a practice, that patient's "knowing you were there" resulted in a number of referrals over the years. And that is one of the more important ways a private practice builds. But short of this sort of consideration, people who enter into psychotherapy with a private therapist expect *continuity of service.* It is implicit in the written or verbal contract with the therapist. And as all of us know, one of the most important needs felt by anyone suffering from depression, anxiety, or any of the disturbed mood states or states of familial or social disorganization is a sense of trust, reliability, and continuity in the person of the helper. Indeed, one of the serious deficits of institutional practice as compared with private practice is the difficulty agencies have in providing continuity. Some agencies ultimately ignore the issue as a problem, or even turn it around and defensively tout the lack of continuity of individual staff as being less important to patients than the superior reliability and continuity of the agency as an institution. That argument may be reasonable when it applies to purchasing cars or television sets, but it is quite silly in relation to psychotherapy, where the substance of the interchange is between two people and involves most intimate matters. And in terms of modern "Self-Psychology" à la Kohut, the concept is disastrous.

Perhaps because social workers have traditionally been employed by agencies and institutions, they have been more persistent and explicit in distinguishing private practice from employment in agencies or proprietary organizations. By their definition, a lawyer who is employed in a private law partnership is technically considered to be an employee rather than a private practitioner. One can go as far as he wishes with this technical definition, for example, even excluding from private practice the chief partners of major law firms or senior partners or officers of professional psychotherapy partnerships or corporations. But for our purposes, the significant distinction, technical or otherwise, is the degree to which the individual practitioner sets the terms and conditions of exchange with his patient, the extent to which he maintains responsibility for his own practice, and, if employed in a proprietary organization, the degree to which he may directly influence its policies and control system.

In the instance where a social worker, for example, is employed by a psychiatrist in a practice that is owned and controlled by the psychiatrist and the psychiatrist retains ultimate "medical responsibility" for all his patients, it would be difficult to consider the social worker to be in private practice, no matter how extensive his "autonomy" in the direct management or treatment of his clients. He would essentially be employed as a psychotherapist in someone else's private practice. The same would be true for a psychiatrist employed by another psychiatrist, a psychologist employed by a psychologist, or either employed by a clinical social worker, another physician or anyone else.

The problem of differentiating between employee status and being in private practice is becoming increasingly difficult. If an independent practitioner incorporates, for example, he becomes an employee of his corporation legally even though he may be its sole owner and its only employee. The distinctions between proprietary and not-for-profit settings are also becoming fuzzier, especially with the increasing prevalence of third party payers in meeting the costs of psychotherapy. Perhaps the discussion in chapter 4 of the solo versus group practice will aid the reader in thinking through what is best for him, which is, after all, the main purpose of this book.

What Distinguishes Private Practice from Employee Status?

Perhaps the three clearest distinctions between employee status and private practice status are (1) the degree of real autonomy in practice, (2) the entrepreneurial responsibilities of the practitioner, and (3) ultimate ownership of the practice. Clearly, the purest form of private practice occurs in the solo practice model. Yet more and more private practice groups are forming throughout the country, and many of these provide essential elements of private practice for their individual members and clients. Without belaboring this complex and conundrum-like matter, let me suggest that each practitioner must evaluate and decide for himself whether he is indeed entering into private practice status or is simply taking another job in the for-profit sector.

Some guidelines to help a practitioner evaluate a position offered to him may be useful. The situation should be one where the therapist will ultimately be on a par with his peers in the control and ownership of the practice. Regular progression toward this status within a specified time frame should be spelled out in writing, together with a clear statement as to where the responsibility for the direct treatment lies. The patient's responsibilities to pay for treatment and opportunity to choose his therapist should be specified in writing. The basic concept is that the practitioner "owns himself" and no one "owns" the patients but themselves.

Credibility

The credibility of a practitioner emerges from going through the process of commitment and is expressed through his feeling of ease and comfort with his decision to be in private practice. Of course, public credibility is increased by one's academic credentials, past and present affiliations with re-spected professional organizations or public institutions, special professional awards, published articles, listing in appro-priate professional registries, community and/or professional activities, and lecturing and teaching. Probably the greatest weight publicly is given to the style, presence, personality, and demeanor of the practitioner as he presents himself.

Yet therapists differ from each other remarkably. Consider the therapist who dresses in up-to-date fashions and is always impeccably groomed and the one who always has hay-seed in his hair and appears just to have stumbled out of a night in the stable even when he's "dressed up." Both may be suc-cessful. The key components that they share are that both have clarity about what they do and how they do it, and have respect for their own ability. Idiosyncracies of dress or other superfi-cial matters fade before this central professional character-istic.

Credibility, as might be guessed, is importantly associated with success in practice, although a number of other attributes may also be identified. Wallace (1977)[25] finds, for example, that psychotherapists who engage in private practice relatively soon after graduate training tend to be more successful in terms of having larger practices. That may simply be a function of longevity in practice; i.e., the longer in practice, the larger the pool of former patients and the larger the source of potential referrals. Or it may be related to the greater readiness of the therapist to assert his competence, confidence, and credibility. It should be noted that nowhere in the Wallace study is there discussion or recommendation of such things as entertaining, sending substantial gifts, and other similar devices to establish credibility or to generate referrals. Reputable and successful therapists rarely require them. Entertaining, gift giving, and otherwise socializing ought to follow the basic rule of honesty and straightforwardness. Now, it is true that there are times when social occasions may become the situs for important communication. But this should best be by-product, not purpose.

This chapter has reviewed the components of readiness for private practice, including acquiring the appropriate academic credentials, licenses, and professional accreditation, supervised experience, personal commitment to engage over a lifetime career in the practice of psychotherapy, commitment to the entrepreneurial aspects of private practice, and credibility based on the genuine confidence that is an outgrowth of competence.

The next chapter discusses ways to develop referrals, probably the most worrisome aspect of private practice for both beginners and experienced people.

CHAPTER 4

Portals of Entry into Psychotherapy and into Private Practice

"An estimated 34 million Americans are receiving professional psychotherapy or counseling, and millions more are believed to be in need of it."

Jane E. Brody in the *Chicago Tribune*, 1981

Without doubt, the most pressing question most therapists will be concerned about after they have committed themselves to entering into private practice is how to build the practice. A useful conceptual umbrella is to consider this matter as one of how to open new portals of entry into psychotherapy for people who need it while simultaneously opening new portals of entry into private practice for therapists who choose to undertake it.

Most experienced therapists have observed that potential clients often have great difficulty finding their way into treatment. And most therapists have great difficulty finding appropriate trustworthy people or institutions to refer patients to. An illustration from medicine of the difficulty in finding one's way into treatment is the following: A colleague reported his anxiety about some physical symptoms he was experiencing. He wanted to have some radiological and blood work done to ease his fears. His office happened to be located in a medical building where a laboratory and radiology center were also located. He knew their staff well. Yet he could not gain entry through their "portals" for diagnostic evaluation simply by walking in. He had to go to his internist to be referred. The internist was the "gatekeeper."

How many people are there who want to see a therapist, perhaps only for evaluation or reassurance, but cannot find a simple, easy portal of entry? Usually, one seeks out a "gatekeeper" like a doctor, lawyer, minister, school principal, or friend to open the door. But what an awesome responsibility for the gatekeeper. How does he find a trustworthy therapist to whom to refer? When even experienced therapists have difficulty, how much more so a layman friend or a professional from another discipline. Within the context of these observations, it appears that the therapists who announce their availability to the gatekeeper in a meaningful honest way are indeed providing them help with making referrals when called upon to do so. The therapist who makes the rounds of potential referral sources is not a mendicant begging for business, but is rather a professional engaged in the process of opening portals of entry into psychotherapy for those who need it.

Gatekeepers and Practice Building

Psychotherapists in private practice around the country report generally that the primary source of referrals is physicians. For those who have been in practice a long time, former patients are the most important source. Another source is professional colleagues, who tend to refer friends, relatives, and others.

Wallace (1977)[26] found that more than half of the social workers he surveyed said that their own clients were their best source of referrals, and an additional 20 percent said they were their second best source. Nevertheless, physicians and hospitals were the most important source for many. Referrals from psychiatrists or other private practitioners ranked next. Wallace says that "*the key to a large practice seems to be having more different sources referring.*" He speculated that practitioners who tend to isolate themselves from the professional community tend to have smaller practices, perhaps because they are turned to by other professionals less frequently. He found further that what practitioners actually do with their clients does not seem related to the size of the practice. Wryly he comments, "Just because he has a big practice does not mean that he is any good." Furthermore, lower fees do not seem to be positively related to size of practice. "The fee for practitioner time from a person with a large practice is . . . 33 percent greater than from a person with a small practice." Wallace concludes that private practitioners act like most professional and business people in that "a greater demand for service results in higher prices for that service. Alternately, individuals attempting to begin practice may make it well-known that they are willing to see cases for a lower fee." If, indeed, the primary sources of one's referrals are one's own patients or professional colleagues, a practitioner who is uncomfortable with fees, worried about referrals, or worried about his clinical judgment will be unlikely to inspire referrals and their correlate, a large practice. As Wallace says, "Who would want surgery from a physician who is nervous, does not like surgery, is insecure about what to charge and wonders where his next case is coming from?"

One's confidence and credibility must be in some way communicated to the professional and general public. Virtually everything that one does in choosing an office and setting it up is part of the process of establishing one's credibility. There are, in addition, several commonly accepted means of becoming known professionally including, among others, offering direct and/or consultation services to community agencies like schools, churches, and businesses or to professionals like social workers, psychologists, psychiatrists, physicians, clergy, teachers, and lawyers; writing professional articles and articles for local public media; activities within the community like school board membership, Rotary, League of Women Voters, church boards, and others; offering to speak to local groups on professionally relevant topics; joining with other colleagues to sponsor forums for professionals or laymen; and affiliating with local hospitals or other institutions.

Selecting an office is part of an ongoing process of introducing one's self to the community and especially to the community "gatekeepers." It is a vital part of the process. By way of illustration, a young woman therapist recently came to talk to an older well-established colleague regarding her initiation of private practice. She had opened an office in the community in which she lived. She said that she had already talked with a number of potential referral sources. One of those who worked in a "high psychotherapy I.Q." suburb nearby told her she ought to open an office in that particular suburb and then he could refer to her. She asked if this was really necessary. The older colleague responded that if she thought referrals from this community might be important to her, then as an entrepreneur she needed to assess the potential economic gain she might expect balanced against the possible inconvenience and the financial and time investment required to open the second office. Let's say that it might cost her $200 a month to maintain the second office. If she charged $50 per session, one per week would pay for her investment of money. The question she needed to ask was how much of a return this extra investment would be worth to her. At the same time, she needed to consider how she wanted to manage her practice, perhaps in relation to her personal needs or wishes. She might decide that her personal needs outweighed the potential increase in her practice that might accrue through opening the second office. This particular "gatekeeper" then might not refer to her, while others would. But if she found that a number of other "gatekeepers" offered similar advice, she might well have to decide differently.

The same young therapist also reported that she had been advised by some colleagues to concentrate her contacts on only a few possible referral sources. The older colleague advised her against that, citing Wallace's survey and his own personal experience that it is far better in the long run to cultivate as many different referral agents as possible. Just as it is unwise to locate one's office in an institution or building that is identified with some particular group, like a church or a single group medical practice, it is unwise to limit one's referral sources. Even when a single medical group of sufficient size might generate enough referrals to fill a practice, one becomes identified with that group and often is automatically cut off from other referral agents. (By the way, this young therapist was doing the right thing by contacting colleagues. She will be in their minds if and when a referral may be appropriate.)

Furthermore, as a general rule, it is advantageous for therapists to move as quickly as possible into a situation where most referrals are generated from one's own former patients and from the community at large rather than from one or more "gatekeepers." This movement may be fostered by the steps discussed below.

One may offer direct service to community agencies on a part-time employment basis, or for dealing with the especially complex problems of certain children, or to do hypnotherapy in selected situations, or to provide psychopharmacological treatment as needed on an hourly set-fee basis. When entering a new community where one is relatively unknown, some such step may be essential as a way of establishing credibility. In addition, through this kind of employment the therapist will have the opportunity to familiarize himself with community resources and other professionals. It is rarely wise to offer to "donate" services to a community agency, even when one is willing to commit a certain amount of time on a rigidly adhered-to schedule. Somehow, the paid agency staff are likely to react negatively, even suspiciously, to such an offer, wondering, "What's in it for this person? Who does this fellow think he is? Is he a carpetbagger?"

The offer is likely to be construed as either grandiose or secretly self-serving. There are, of course, exceptions to this rule, as, for instance, when an unexpected calamity strikes a community, e.g., a hotel fire or collapse, or a train wreck or a devastating tornado. Other exceptions might be where the therapist openly expresses his need for certain case experience in connection with an advanced training program or a special research effort. Another variation that may sometimes be acceptable and even desirable is to offer sharply reduced fees for service to certain agency patients who might otherwise not be able to obtain help because of agency waiting lists or the patient's unique needs.

Obviously, some of the same conditions hold in relation to an offer of consultation to agency staff, to personnel in community schools, churches, businesses, or to other professionals. As an entrepreneur one may offer consultation services at no cost or at a low fee as a way of introducing one's self so long as it is clearly understood that this is a way of building a practice and that the offer is therefore time-limited. Of course, there may be occasions where an institution cannot ever expect to pay for consultation and the therapist may offer it on an ongoing basis as a continuing means of building his practice or to maintain his own intellectual interest. Offers of free consultation even where most openly and benignly made must be handled with great sensitivity and delicacy. After all, the experience of the ancient Greeks with the Trojan horse, which gave rise to the historic adage "Beware of Greeks bearing gifts," probably informs most of us to this day. Charging a reasonable fee for consultation is likely to be much more appropriate and satisfactory for all. Naturally, an offer of consultation implies that one has sufficient expertise to give consultees something of value. Usually, special training, long experience, and specific planning for consultations are a sine qua non if they are to accomplish the purpose of establishing credibility and reputation. While some people welcome consultation, others are put off by it unless they actively seek it on their own initiative. While this is not the place to discuss the intricacies of consultation technique and practice, one basic principle ought to be restated, namely, that the consultees retain control and responsibility for what they do and the consultant is at best an adjunctive helper.

Another avenue for generating referrals is through participation in seminars, workshops, peer-group supervision sessions, and similar activities with other mental health professionals or, even more usefully, with other kinds of professionals. Psychiatrists may find easier access to regular meetings of other medical colleagues, but psychologists and clinical social workers may also arrange to be invited to such sessions. The advantages of this kind of participation in gaining recognition within the gatekeeper community are self-evident. Once again, sensitivity and tact are immensely helpful characteristics in these situations. "No one likes a smart-mouth" is an admonition mental health practitioners must keep in mind in commenting on case presentations involving professionals of other disciplines, especially when psychosocial factors may be evident but ignored by others. Somehow, psychotherapists are often reacted to by others with suspicion, fear, and discomfort. Perhaps this is a corollary to society's mystification, mythologizing, and stereotyping of emotional disturbances and of those who profess to deal with them.

A similar caveat applies to psychotherapists who participate on community boards and committees. Many community groups express love-hate responses to psychotherapists among them. The expertise and occasional wisdom tend to be sought after and simultaneously feared. The sensitive psychotherapist is most likely to impress others with his wisdom when he exercises restraint in advertising it. Focusing on the tasks of the groups and leaving psychotherapeutic insights out of sight may be the best policy.

On the other hand, seeking out opportunities to speak as an expert to community organizations on selected topics of special interest is an excellent way to exhibit professional knowledge and skill and to establish public credibility as an expert. Most organizations welcome speakers, especially from the hometown, who charge little or no fee. Professional women's groups, church groups, PTA, Rotary, Lions, Altrusa, and others are almost always open to interesting programs. A telephone call to the president or the program chairman followed by a brief resume and a cover letter describing a few topics on which one is prepared to speak will usually draw a favorable response. It has been estimated that whenever one speaks to a group of 25 or more, at least two referrals within the following 12 months are generated on the average. Sometimes one is amazed to have a person seeking treatment call and explain that a friend or relative heard a speech and this is how he or she was referred. Speeches to lay groups should rarely extend beyond 25 minutes, but should leave at least 30 minutes for questions and discussion. Psychologically, these presentations represent a "giving" to the group—first by speaking, then by listening. The giving is more important than any "impressing." Of course, good looks, charm, and a sense of humor go a long way toward gaining acceptance. But the substance of one's presentation is most important of all. The hallmarks of a good presentation by a mental health professional are honesty, and forthrightness, with no punches pulled even on controversial topics. For example, there are certainly important groups who have powerful opinions about such matters as birth control, abortion, equal rights for women and minorities, homosexuality, Medicaid, and other welfare programs. Psychotherapists tend as a group to be "liberal" on such matters, possibly as a result of their general orientation of openness and acceptance toward their patients, so many of whom are apt to be socially "different." A wise therapist might not provocatively introduce such topics when addressing a Moral Majority meeting, but he must certainly be honest and head-on in confronting them if they are brought up. Therapists count among their successful treatment cases work with fundamentalist ministers and their families, who tend to test the therapist's beliefs quite vigorously, and to enter into work with him only when they are satisfied that they have been answered honestly. And of course we all know that despite strongly professed beliefs within certain groups, there will always be some group members or members of their families whose behavior will be at odds with the expressed group beliefs. They are likely to want to find an accepting therapist to help them deal with their personal crises away from their own group. Two final caveats: never talk down to a group, and always try to tailor the talk to the group.

Still another way of "advertising" one's self within the format of providing a service is to reproduce (with permission) helpful articles by others or by one's self on mental health topics, with one's own name and a brief statement of one's services attached. These reproductions may be distributed in physician's offices, lawyer's offices, churches, libraries, and hospital waiting rooms. Again, one should have the permission of the professionals lest he feel that he's being exploited for an implied endorsement without being talked to. Parents, grandparents, and teachers are generally grateful to have some guidance in selecting toys, games, books, etc., for children of specific ages, and a simple but well-thought-out article on this subject to be printed in a local newspaper and further distributed, as described above, will help gain one name-recognition. Other topics of interest often are special problems like anorexia, bedwetting, the use of drugs in depression, teen-parent problems, marital problems, problem solving in second marriages with two or more sets of children, mid-career conflicts, and relationships between adult children and aging parents.

Any of these topics would also provide excellent material for local community forums or workshops that could be planned, developed, and sponsored by a local group of mental health professionals. For a professional attempting to build a practice, participation and leadership in such programs is easily recognized as helpful. Or one may offer to work with nonprofessional community groups to arrange programs like these.

Psychiatrists especially will find affiliation with local hospitals and medical societies an important practice builder. Recently, psychologists and clinical social workers too have worked out affiliations with hospitals and clinics that are mutually beneficial. Opening up such affiliations to nonmedical specialists is not only useful to the practitioner, but opens up freedom to choose among various practitioners for the patient. According to the *Wall Street Journal* doctors and non-M.D.s are suing hospitals in greater numbers in order to gain staff privileges. "What's at stake isn't simply the supply and demand of medical services. Open-staff privileges also mean therapist choice for the patient."[27]

Finally, it must be stressed that there is great value in communicating what one does, one's expertise, and one's availability to one's own personal physician and physicians attending family members; to one's attorney, one's minister, and one's children's teachers and school principal; and, of course, to friends, relatives, and neighbors. Even where a therapist does not care to treat friends or neighbors, he may help refer them elsewhere, and in turn they may tell others about him. Practice building is not an easy process, nor should one expect it to occur in a short time. In smaller communities where referral networks are relatively simple and communication through word of mouth is relatively fast, a practice may be solidified within one or two years. In more complex urban centers, it may take a little longer.

Practitioners have used a variety of approaches to expanding or diversifying their practice. Some give pre- and post-surgery counseling to women at local hospitals. Others have turned the experience of their own divorce and remarriage into a business—developing and marketing cassettes "for the newly singled." To overcome the confining aspects of the label "psychotherapist," some present themselves as offering "human-behavior services" which may be applicable to conflict resolution programs in industry, mid-career planning for executives, and so on. Some psychologists whose professional image has been narrowly confined to psychological testing, but who have therapeutic skills and want to reflect that in their image, may make the effort to change it even at the expense of giving up some of their existing business, testing. Mark Lewin advises, "Focus your efforts on one target at a time, and you'll be surprised at how new business begins to come."[28]

One therapist who was skilled in using short-term procedures to cope with stress also had an interest in, and an ability to relate to, athletes. He successfully extended his practice in the area of helping top-level athletes achieve optimal performance. Another such practitioner is a psychologist who also owns a seat on the commodities exchange. His knowledge of the stresses of that occupation has led him to build a practice almost exclusively of people involved with commodities, options, and the stock exchange.

Building a private practice is like many business-oriented marketing procedures. One's goals need to be thought out and approached carefully, slowly, and thoughtfully. The key to success is likely to be a healthy recognition of the fact that you are in business and must try to apply businesslike approaches.

There are varying opinions about whether it is best to present oneself as narrowly specialized or as a generalist.

Most new practices tend to welcome any kind of referral. Many children's therapists can tolerate working with only so many children and want to leaven their practice with adults and families. On the other hand, some therapists prefer specializing in a few specially identified areas within which they feel most competent. Obviously, everyone needs to develop clear objectives related to what they best like to do.

Some therapists have been active in starting self-help groups, such as Parents Without Partners, AA, Widow-to-Widow, and Parents Anonymous (for child abusers). They may serve on the board or as paid or unpaid consultants, and may even refer their patients to such groups. In this way, they may generate referrals to themselves eventually.

And, of course, some simple common-sense steps to take are informing present and former teachers, colleagues in places of employment, and fellow students about entering the arena of private practice.

Alternative Ways of Initiating Practice

Alternative ways of initiating practice are (1) to purchase an existing practice, (2) to enter into a practice with an established therapist, (3) to join a group practice, or (4) to initiate one's practice oneself. Each of these has its advantages and disadvantages.

The advantages of solo practice seem to be these: (1) The solo practitioner enjoys his independence and feels unencumbered by the weight of demands for time or discussion by colleagues. (2) The patient who comes to the solo practitioner feels that the therapist will respect and enhance his sense of individuality in this computer age, and the fact that he has to relate to only one person demands less of him. (3) Group practitioners tend to become ingrown (somewhat like fraternity members), whereas solo practitioners seek contact with a wide range of people. (4) The overhead expense may be less in solo practice than in group practice.

The disadvantages of solo practice in a sense contradict the advantages. They are as follows: (1) Solo practice is, almost by definition, lonely and isolated. (2) It is more difficult to refer certain patients or to collaborate in the treatment of a family in which two or more therapists ought to be involved. (3) It is difficult to get help in covering a practice when the therapist goes on vacation or needs to be away from his practice for any emergency. (4) There is no one with whom to share overhead expenses, such as secretarial and telephone-answering services, and waiting room equipment.

Some of the advantages of group or partnership practice are: (1) There is a greater opportunity for individual practitioners to specialize. (2) A group or partnership can often carry more weight in community activities and in action on political and social policy matters. (3) The group or partnership may become known as a general resource that is always available in the community. (4) The group or partnership can effectively cover professional meetings and conventions by arranging for one or more members to attend and report back to the rest. (5) There may be some savings in group insurance plans and other overhead matters. (6) There is opportunity for referrals back and forth.

Disadvantages to group or partnership practice are as follows: (1) It is not easy to find a number of professional people who can work easily and comfortably together. (2) Usually there is a complicated administrative job to be done that demands someone's time. (3) There may be a loss of privacy for the patient and the practitioner.[29] (4) There may actually be an increase in overhead expense. (5) Practice-building efforts by individual members are likely to be just as necessary and time-consuming as in a solo practice.

Some of the factors one needs to consider if one is planning a group practice include the qualifications, interests, and specialized skills of those who might associate themselves together; community needs; office space needs (and allocation); equipment requirements; initial capital requirements; division of costs, income, time, and responsibility; the possible need to borrow capital; legal arrangements regarding partnership or limited incorporation or full incorporation; and probable attitudes of other professionals toward establishment of such a group.

Interprofessional group practice may involve partnerships or corporations (where state law permits) which include several different professions, such as social workers, physicians, lawyers, and psychologists. Most of what was said about establishing a group practice applies to interprofessional group practice. Additional problems that need to be worked through include questions of status, for example, between psychiatrists, psychologists, and social workers. A carefully thought-out written agreement will help all parties establish for themselves and each other the extent and limitations of responsibility of each professional person in regard to professional matters involving the treatment of the client and business arrangements. Fee splitting, even in a disguised form, is considered an unethical practice and certainly must be guarded against in this kind of group practice. Payments into the group for overhead expenses, such as rent or consultation by a senior member to a junior should be realistic rather than artifically inflated for the profit of the senior.

Informal relationships may develop between some clinicians and groups of pediatricians, obstetricians, psychiatrists, and others that are essentially referral arrangements rather than formal partnerships

Whatever the form of a group practice, it is of the essence that the individual practitioner maintain direct professional responsibility for the treatment of his patients. One of the problems that tends to be fostered by the differential treatment by third-party payers (mostly insurance companies) of the several psychotherapy professions regarding fee reimbursements is the employment of clinical social workers and clinical psychologists by psychiatrists and other physicians, where the clinical social worker or psychologist does the work while the psychiatrist "signs off" the insurance claim and collects the fee. In those states where psychologists have won the right to third party coverage, they too have engaged in the employment of social workers and others in a similar way. Many professionals and insurance companies object to this practice, since it tends to inflate fees, and may in fact represent a form of fee splitting. Many think that if it is not clearly a corrupt practice, it may, at the very least, appear to be and may affect the credibility of the therapist with the patient and with the community. It is a practice that tends to demean clinical social workers and psychologists. Rarely is it a practice that protects the patient-consumer or the third-party payer or the community. More often it is simply an economically motivated arrangement that is the product of political action by professional organizations and that is in general not socially desirable.

Relatively few psychotherapists are in partnerships, although many therapists investigate the idea. The truth is, partnerships are difficult financially, professionally, and personally.

Two examples follow. A therapist had been in private practice about five years and found that he had a surplus of referrals. At about the same time, an old friend and colleague grew tired of his administrative duties in an agency. The first therapist encouraged the second to enter into private practice, assuring him that he would make appropriate introductions to "gatekeepers" and that he would be able to make a substantial number of referrals himself. To avoid endangering their friendship or complicating it, they agreed not to form a partnership. Furthermore, they saw that there would be greater mutual advantages accruing through the second fellow's establishing himself independently but within the same community. The arrangement worked well and was professionally synergistic for both for a number of years. Eventually, however, the former administrator received a new administrative job offer "that he couldn't refuse." They worked jointly to dissolve his practice and arrange for the continuing care of some of his patients. All of this was accomplished informally and comfortably to everyone's satisfaction.

The second illustration shows what may go wrong. In this instance the well-established practitioner drew up a formal agreement within which he guaranteed a younger therapist a certain number of referrals. The older man was responsible for paying the younger a proportion of the fee for each treatment session he conducted. The remaining proportion of the fee was to go for overhead expenses. The proportion of the total fee to be paid to the younger man was to increase according to an agreed-upon formula related to the actual overhead costs until the younger man would be receiving his full fees less actual costs. A serious financial error was incorporated in this plan. The more "successful" the new therapist became, the greater grew the amount of "accounts receivable" owing to the first therapist. That is, the second man was paid monthly for the therapy sessions he held, but there was always at least one month's lag in collecting actual fees from his patients. At the end of several years, several thousand dollars was owing. The problem was resolved by canceling the previous agreement and going to a 50/50 split on all expenses with the second man taking over collection of his lagging fees and paying them off to the first over a period of a year or so as if they were a debt. They are still good friends, work closely together, and find this arrangement as independent practitioners who only share overhead expenses most satisfactory. They are able to purchase certain insurances together under a favorable arrangement. Because of differences in their ages and personal circumstances they do not encumber each other in regard to retirement plans as would be the case if they were in formal partnership. They could have avoided the difficult debt burden incurred by the younger man and the irritating "accounts receivable" problem incurred by the older had they planned more carefully in advance with the advice of a management consultant.

Other experiments with partnerships bear out the caveats with regard to the need for compatibility of personalities and of professional style or approaches to treatment. For most, the advantages of freedom of action as an independent solo practitioner only loosely affiliated with other practitioners outweigh the advantages of a formal partnership or corporate arrangement.

If a partnership or group practice is decided upon, it is absolutely essential to employ specialized professional consultants, including a management consultant, an accountant, and preferably lawyers to represent each of the proposed partners. This planning experience itself may help therapists to decide whether to go ahead with it or not to do so.

Building a practice is not easy but it is feasible. Most therapists who have done it on their own find it preferable to joining a partnership or a group practice. The informal relationships they build with colleagues tend to suit their needs best.

In the next chapter, consideration is given to beginning the practice.

CHAPTER 5

Choosing a Location and Setting Up an Office

Planning for private practice is a creative process that fosters development of commitment.

AFTER A PROFESSIONAL has done some hard thinking about whether to enter into private practice, he may be ready to consider the question, "How do I begin?" Some of the issues he may consider are: "Shall I join an existing practice group or go it alone as a solo practitioner?" "Should I seek out a practice that's for sale or begin my own?"

Since each of us is different, some of us are attracted to beginning things ourselves, while others are just as well pleased to enter into a preexisting setting. Whatever the personal preferences, one is in a better position to evaluate and decide after having considered the steps involved in beginning and establishing a solo practice. In this chapter and the next, the process will be reviewed.

The elements involved in beginning a private practice include:

1. Choosing the community (or communities) in which to practice

2. Selecting an office

3. Considering and negotiating leases or other contracts and costs

4. Placement of signs, heat, and air conditioning; cleaning service, hours the building is open and heated

5. Design and furnishing of an office; soundproofing

6. Telephone and telephone-answering systems

7. Announcements and other advertising

8. Stationery, billing forms, and business cards

Choosing a Community

The location of an office is likely to affect the nature of one's practice significantly. Clients tend to seek services that are geographically close and accessible. Referral sources tend to feel more comfortable referring to a professional who is felt to be part of their own community or at least close to it. Easy accessibility is obviously important, especially if one works with children, adolescents, older people, or the handicapped. Public transportation, availability of parking, security and safety, and privacy are all important. The *Handbook of Private Practice of Social Work* sums up various aspects of choosing an office location as follows:

> Since American metropolitan areas tend to be segregated by race, social class, and other socio-economic factors, office location may tend to encourage development of a practice that is segregated racially, culturally, or socially, or it may tend to encourage a broad spectrum of clients. . . . In most cities, there are special sections, usually in the downtown area, devoted to professional offices. Often such locations are relatively impersonal, and a [psychotherapist] planning to open a practice there ought

to have substantial sources of referral and professional contacts well in advance. There are, however, many advantages to such a location, since it permits easy access to other professional people, centers for professional education and meetings, and to a client population that may come from all sections of the city. . . .

In the suburban or downtown urban or rural community, an office located in a building occupied by other professionals, such as physicians, psychiatrists, and attorneys is most likely to provide the dignity, routine service and maintenance, and other amenities. . . . To locate in a private school, church or other institution may tend to associate the practitioner with that institution in the eyes of the clients and the community.[30]

Choosing to locate in a storefront obviously has other implications for a practice, both positive and negative. On the positive side, it is likely to be easily accessible, especially to clients who might not otherwise enter an office. On the negative side, it is likely to discourage middle- and upper-middle-class patients.

Preliminary considerations regarding the selection of an office site or community in which to practice should include, of course, what kind of practice one wishes to pursue. Here, for example, is one therapist's arrangement. He has two office locations. One is in a suburban community, and the other is in the Chicago Loop, the downtown commercial section. The location of these two offices has led to the development of two quite different practices. In the suburban office this therapist tends to see young married couples, some children and adolescents, and an increasing number of aged people. Sprinkled in that practice, of course, are a number of single or divorced young men and women holding professional positions in nursing, teaching, social work, accounting, and so on. His Loop location, on the other hand, has tended to lead to the development of a practice consisting almost exclusively of adults. The majority of the people referred to him there are in the age range of the early twenties through middle age. The bulk of the Loop practice consists of professionals—lawyers, dentists, social workers, psychologists, physicians, and so on. These differences are not accidental. The office locations have a great deal to do with the difference in the two practices. In the Loop location referrals tend to come from the entire Chicago metropolitan area, but most especially referrals come from people living in the city who are middle-class and able to pay private therapy fees. In the suburbs, most referrals are through word of mouth, from client to client. A substantially larger portion of the Loop practice is referred by professional colleagues who know the therapist personally.

He chose to open a private practice office in a south suburb of Chicago because he was already quite well known in that suburban community. Secondly, he knew that that community was not served by many professional psychotherapists. Further, he knew that there was an extensive market for such services in the south suburban area. The overall population was dense, running into several hundred thousand people. The number of therapists in the area was limited, less than five or six at that time. There was only one family agency serving the entire population (in addition to services in the city offered by sectarian agencies at least an hour away). There was a large unserved market. Finally, he chose to open an office in the south suburbs because his home was located there, and therefore it was especially convenient for him and for his family.

However, when one lives in the suburbs and has one's office there, one tends to feel somewhat removed from the hub of professional activities, usually located in the central city. It was with this in mind that he determined to open a private practice in the downtown area. He was not aware at the time that this would lead to the development of different kinds of practices. His intention was to place himself in a situation where he would have contact with other professionals and with professional activities, meetings, etc.

For a practitioner considering practice in rural or small communities, it would seem appropriate to think about the possibility of having more than one office location. That is, if one lives in a community of, say, a population of 25,000 and there are a number of other therapists already practicing in the community, one might consider opening a second office in another community, smaller or even larger. In deciding on an office location in a rural or small community, one ought to consider the availability of transportation and patterns of travel, communication, and shopping. Is the community one where people from farms or other rural areas tend to congregate? In sparsely populated areas, a 50- to 100-mile round trip for an appointment is not likely to be considered unreasonable. If a patient who lives or works in a suburb decides to see a therapist in the Chicago Loop, the appointment arrangement may well require an hour's travel to and from (two hours altogether) plus the time for the session. One can find out a great deal about patterns of shopping, transportation, etc., simply by talking with local chambers of commerce, Rotary Club members, and professionals and merchants in the communities under consideration.

The specific office site that this therapist chose in the suburbs is in a community that is geographically near the center of the population concentrations of the south suburban Chicago area and in a building that caters to professionals. The Loop location is in as central a place as possible and in a building that is primarily used by physicians, attorneys, psychiatrists, psychologists, and social workers. One problem that at least partly results from the location of the suburban office in an almost completely white middle-class community has been that very few black patients have sought his help. A substantial part of his Loop practice, on the other hand, consists of black and other minority patients.

It bears repeating that in choosing an office location, one ought to keep in mind what kind of practice one wants to have. For example, if one is planning to specialize in the treatment of children and adolescents, a suburban or a rural location is likely to be the most desirable. If one wants to work with young, single, white-collar or professional patients, one ought to locate in a major downtown city area. Obviously, since demographics and urban ecology vary from place to place throughout the country, one will need to consider specific community patterns.

Another consideration in choosing a particular community in which to practice and an office location might be the degree of growth, or lack of growth, of population, industry, and commerce in the area. For example, at the time this book is being written, the southwestern part of the United States seems to be the area where there is the greatest population, industrial, and commercial growth in the country. A piece of advice to a psychotherapist choosing a specific office would be, if at all possible, to locate in an office building that is relatively newly opened and into which are moving physicians, lawyers, and other professionals who are also in the process of opening their practices at the same time that he is. For one thing, this provides a mutual core of shared experience around which the therapist may communicate and upon which he may build professional as well as social relationships. Through those kinds of relationships he is likely to receive referrals as well as to be in a position to make referrals to others.

A further consideration in choosing a community in which to locate is the degree of comfort the therapist is likely to feel being there. For example, not many prep school WASPs are likely to feel comfortable locating in Spanish Harlem. Nor is a black therapist, no matter how competent, likely to feel comfortable in an all-white suburb. Where possible, locating in an integrated area or in a commercial area that caters to a broad-spectrum population is likely to be the most suitable choice for most therapists. However, a therapist of a particular ethnic or racial background may consciously choose to locate in an area where he can serve his particular ethnic or racial group.

Some further considerations may enter into choosing a community. If one is personally well known in a community, that will help to build a practice. Of course, some therapists may feel a loss of anonymity, but on balance, the advantages of being well known outweigh the disadvantages. The community, however, should be large enough to provide a market for one's services. A rough estimate of potential users of psychotherapy in a community might be 2 percent per year. In a community of 25,000, for example, as many as 500 people a year might seek some kind of help. Naturally, communities vary significantly in relation to their "psychotherapy I.Q.," or readiness to seek psychotherapy. Studies indicate that most consumers of psychotherapy are in the 18- to 55-year-old age range, come from families who have above average education, and hold white-collar, managerial, or professional jobs. Obviously, communities with substantial populations like these would be more likely to support a practice. Paradoxically, communities where other therapists have already located are likely to be more productive than a psychotherapy wasteland, provided that there is not an oversupply of therapists. Generally, it is easier to establish a practice in a community that is growing rather than standing still or shrinking.

Overall, one needs to think through the kind of practice one wants to establish and the kind of community within which one is likely to feel comfortable personally.

Selecting an Office

Selection of a specific office site is a somewhat easier task than choosing the community. A practitioner has four general options: (1) an office at home, (2) use of an office in an agency, hospital, church, or similar institution, (3) sublease of space from another professional, (4) leasing or buying his own office, and (5) renting space on an equal basis with another therapist.

Each of these options has its advantages and disadvantages. An office at home is likely to be less expensive and offers some tax advantages. It is convenient, and the therapist may be more readily available to his family in emergencies or for special events. Work time may be more flexibly scheduled around family activities. And there may be a more homey ambiance that some patients find less threatening. For encounter groups, "re-parenting," and similar approaches, one's home may be the location of choice.

There are, however, the disadvantages of greater difficulty in maintaining one's family's and one's own privacy, as well as the client's. Soundproofing a private residence is difficult and expensive. One's family may feel rivalrous, deprived, and angry at the therapist closeting with patients, seemingly in preference to them. Children especially find this difficult to accept, although there are therapists who actively involve their families as part of the therapeutic milieu. Clients may feel guilty about invading the therapist's privacy while simultaneously resenting not being a real "insider." Sometimes, though thankfully rarely, there is a possible risk of physical assault on one's self or one's family from a decompensated patient. And finally, an office at home may contribute to professional isolation.

One therapist described his experience in beginning his practice in a basement office in his home. His children were young. He used the office on Saturdays and evenings, just those times when the children were home. Somehow it was at just those times that the worst squabbles broke out, the most painful or bloody accidents occurred, and general mayhem ensued. The therapist found that he was often distracted, his clients dismayed, and his wife distraught. Everyone was greatly relieved when he took a small office away from home. (Other therapists, of course, might have seen these "interferences" as opportunities for therapeutic work.)

One final note: Some communities restrict the use of a residence for business or professional practice. Condominiums and apartment buildings also may have restrictive regulations. Obviously, one must look into these possibilities when considering an office at home.

Using an office in an agency or other institution has its advantages and disadvantages too. If one is on staff or otherwise employed in a hospital or clinic, it is certainly convenient and probably less expensive to use one's own office there to see private patients part-time. Books, papers, records, equipment, and so on are consolidated and available. In some instances the practitioner's credibility may be enhanced by the association with a well-respected community institution. And often it is a convenience to the agency and the client to have the practitioner so readily available.

There are, however, potential disadvantages. For one, to what extent is the private work distinguished from the institutional job? Will patients feel better or worse that they may be mistaken for a clinic patient? What steps does the practitioner take to guard against the appearance or the reality of conflicts of interest? For example, when a patient has sought help from a not-for-profit clinic within which a therapist's office is located and for one reason or another is referred to the therapist privately, how can the patient and the community be assured that basically the referral is not simply for the therapist's benefit, rather than for the patient's?

Taking an office in a church has advantages and disadvantages. It may encourage self-referrals and referrals from clergy and church members because some sanction by the church probably is implied. On the other hand, the therapist may be perceived by the community at large as identified with the one particular denomination, and outsiders may feel discouraged. In addition, some patients may feel threatened by guilt associated with anything church-related. And finally, some people may find it confusing that someone practicing out of their church charges substantial fees.

Nowadays, with optical, dental, legal, and other professional practices located within major retail chains like Sears, psychotherapy practices may soon follow. Making therapy more readily accessible to patients would certainly be desirable. It is not clear what the possible disadvantages will be. But this may be an interesting new service delivery development during the 1980s.

In any event, arrangements to use agency or institutional offices for private practice should always, without exception, be specified clearly in writing, preferably in the shape of a formal contract. This may save incalculable pain arising from misunderstanding later.

Probably the way psychotherapists most often begin their practices is by subleasing space from another professional—another psychotherapist, a doctor, dentist, lawyer, or some other professional. While this course of action seems relatively the easiest, experience suggests pitfalls about which to be wary. A therapist needs to "lay claim" to his office space in order to increase his sense of security and comfort. This is often difficult when subleasing. For example, one male therapist initially sublet space from a woman therapist. The office was pleasant and was located in a prestigious professional office building. However, he never felt comfortable there, and his landlord was unhappy too. The furnishings were too "feminine" for his taste, and the lingering odor of his pipe smoke offended the woman therapist. In addition, the male therapist saw a number of children, and their toys and models disrupted the decor. Eventually these two parted friends, agreeing that their arrangement just had more drawbacks than pluses. Sometimes there are even more difficult problems in subleasing. For example, where the landlord is an M.D. and the lessee is a psychologist or clinical social worker, status issues may become a problem, particularly when the landlord does not want the tenant's name to appear on the door or on the building directory, as sometimes happens. Nevertheless, older established therapists often want to encourage and help younger practitioners to get started and may offer to sublet space on unusually favorable terms. In every instance, including the latter, terms should be spelled out in writing, with hours, cost, privileges, identifying signs, and use of phone and phone-answering services all specified. Once again, putting it in writing can save grief later, and whatever the long-range outcome, from the start it is likely to preserve a good relationship between tenant and landlord rather than injure it. In addition, formulating a contract helps the therapist solidify his commitment to enter into private practice. The decision becomes more "real" and binding.

One further comment about subleasing. It is vital that the professional who holds the lease clear with the building owner before entering into a sublease. Naturally, this is not necessary when the building is owned by the professional. It is necessary, however, if the building is owned by a corporation or partnership of which the "landlord" professional is one member, to clear it with the other partner or corporate members.

Another way to begin is to rent an office in an equal partnership with another professional therapist. Some of the same caveats listed above apply here. Most important of all is that *a written agreement be worked out in advance* between the partners above and beyond whatever agreements are worked out with the landlord. There are many advantages to this kind of partnership, such as reduction of overhead costs. One may be able to afford better secretarial and telephone services, for example, in addition to other amenities that would be difficult if one went solo. But partnerships, like marriages and all other human relationships, are fraught with problems, conflicts, and disagreements along with pleasures and bonuses. The "odd couple" syndrome demonstrates both the deficits and pluses and illustrates the work necessary to maintain such relationships. While therapists may be excellent at helping other "odd couples" work out their difficulties, they are as vulnerable as any others to suffering from, as well as enjoying, the human condition.

Office Selection as a Practice-building Process

Probably the simplest and "cleanest" way to get an office is to lease one independently. There may be compromises in regard to size and furnishings, but these are not likely to be as problematic as the complexities involved in any of the other arrangements. In real estate it is often said that "location is everything." The location of an office is likely to be more important than its size or physical beauty. One excellent way to gain initial recognition in a community and to "announce" one's self is through contacting the "gatekeepers" in the community to get their advice about where to locate an office. The gatekeepers for referrals are other psychotherapists, physicians, social workers, clergymen, school staff, clinic and hospital staff, social agency personnel, lawyers, police, public health nurses, community leaders, elected officials, personnel managers, and business people. Generally it's more comfortable to approach them for information about the community—especially about office location in relation to accessibility for all segments of the potential client population, about the reputation of respective building locations, and even about other professionals—than it is to ask them directly to make referrals. Usually they are flattered to be approached. It gives the psychotherapist a chance to present himself and explain what he does and what his concerns are in a way that is not threatening to them or to himself. It gives them a chance to size the therapist up within a neutral context on their turf. And when he finally does open his office, he will have natural entree to contact them again to tell them what he's doing and that he's there, "open for business."

Naturally, it helps for a therapist to present himself intelligently in relation to the office selection process. He would do well to make preliminary explorations on his own regarding what's available, make his own observations of traffic patterns, etc. It is well not to appear either "all-knowing" or completely "unknowing," but somewhere in-between—a thoughtful person who asks reasonable but not impossible questions. The questions about accessibility, quality of the buildings and neighborhoods, etc. outlined above are a good guide. And he need not worry about not having a business card already prepared to leave with the "gatekeepers" he contacts. Most of us throw them away anyway. What is important is to have the door open for future contacts in a relaxed way. Each of these contacts, by the way, should be limited in time to no more than half an hour even if the other person is willing to be more generous. These contacts are also a good time to plant the seed of one's potential usefulness as a "free" speaker or discussion leader for institutions or organizations in which the gatekeeper may be interested.

The kind of practice one expects to have will determine the specific kind of office space desired. Architecture does tend to have a heavy impact on the way we live our lives personally and professionally. Even the color of walls and furnishings is important. Generally, the office should be comfortable for the practitioner, although if his preferences lean toward the very unusual or bizarre, it might be well to seek consultation. Mirrored ceilings or froufrou drapes and carpeting may be too much even for a client who is otherwise rendered oblivious by his own anxieties. An office that is small and windowless may be too claustrophobic and might discourage seeing families or small groups, while a larger space may encourage this kind or practice. Too elegant an office may discourage work with children, while an office on a second floor or higher, with no elevator, may rule out work with handicapped, elderly, or possibly certain phobic patients. All of us interact with space. Preplanning of remodeling and furnishings will give more control over the space available.

Nothing, of course, is perfect, and compromises will no doubt be necessary. Nevertheless, this brief review will be useful to the new practitioner in thinking through his selection process. Next for consideration are some specifics for leases, rentals, or buying an office.

Negotiating a Lease

The final stages of selecting an office involve some of the more mundane matters like negotiating cost, lease or other contracts, arranging soundproofing, placement of signs, heating, and air conditioning, cleaning services, hours the building is open, heated, and/or locked, and security. In all of these matters it is well to remember that almost all issues are negotiable between tenant and landlord, but the landlord is much more experienced and wiser about them than the renter is likely to be. One considers the reputation of the dealer when shopping for and ultimately purchasing a car or any other major item, and one should do the same when shopping for office space, whether it is to be in a small community or in a huge city complex.

Cost

Office space is usually rented on a cost per square foot per year basis, and the charges may vary from as little as $3 per square foot to as much as $15 per square foot. This way of computing rental cost means the following: Let us say the space to be rented is a 12 × 12 interviewing room and an 8 × 12 waiting/reception room. The total square footage is 144 square feet (12 × 12) plus 96 square feet (8 × 12), or 240 square feet in all. If the price charged per square foot is $10, the rental will be 240 times $10, or $2,400 per year, divided by 12 months, $200 per month. Most of us are primarily interested in that monthly rental cost, but the square foot cost is a useful measure to compare the relative value of one office with another. Space in relatively modern buildings located in or near large metropolitan communities that include in the rent central heating, air conditioning, and regular cleaning service rarely cost less than $10 per square foot per year. A recent Commerce Department report said the national average for office rent is $1.33 per square foot per month, or almost $16 per square foot per year. Landlords will negotiate these prices but will rarely reduce them unless there is a glut of office space on the market, and that is not generally the case. Landlords' policies will vary in regard to allocation of costs for remodeling space to suit a tenant. In buildings under construction, they may build space to suit at no additional cost. In existing buildings, they may expect the renter to pay part or all of the cost of remodeling, but may spread the cost by adding it to the monthly rent over a number of years. For example, the cost of remodeling might be $2,000. Spread over three years the monthly cost would be $55. If the lease were for three years at $200 per month plus $55 extra per month, the total rental would be $255 per month.

A best bet, of course, is to find an office that has already been remodeled for someone else who has moved out. All that may need to be done then is some minor remodeling.

The major remodeling required by psychotherapists usually is soundproofing. Generally, the keys to soundproofing are (1) installing double walls, especially between waiting room and interviewing room, and being sure that they extend the full height from floor to structural ceiling (not false ceiling), and (2) installing a solid-core door (a "psychiatric door") that is weather-stripped on all four sides. Most sound travels through spaces around doors, through false or cosmetic ceilings, and through air ducts that are not baffled. Sometimes a less satisfactory solution is to install a "gray-sound" device in the waiting/reception room that "covers" any other conversational sound from the interview room. It is best not to take the landlord's word on soundproofing, since he may not thoroughly understand a therapist's requirements. It is better to discuss the problem with building contractors who have already done similar work for other therapists, or to hire an acoustical engineer consultant, or to discuss it with other therapists who have already been through the process and from whose mistakes one may profit. In general, it is better to skimp on almost anything else, except air conditioning, than on soundproofing. And it is essential to investigate soundproofing yourself and to follow up directly on its installation personally.

In relation to air conditioning, one must think not only of temperature but of volume of air flow. Most builders do not take into consideration the special conditions of therapy, where the interviewing room is literally sealed shut for long periods of time. Preferably, control of the office temperature should be located within the office.

There are five other matters that are often overlooked in planning: (1) having a window, (2) a sink, (3) adequate storage space for equipment, supplies, etc., and separate space for a clothes closet—in both cases, space that is secure, (4) adequate storage and play space that can be easily walled off, for work with children and/or storage for extra chairs or pillows for work with larger groups, and (5) lighting. (Flourescent lights are to be avoided at all costs. They are cold, distracting, even depressing, and often noisy. Floor or hanging lamps are warmer and more flexible.)

One colleague reported that he spent more than three years working in a windowless office. It became unbearable after a few hours, disorienting and depressing. Even if the blinds are drawn over windows most of the time, the availability of a window is essential.

Secondly, a sink, or at least a water cooler is really an essential luxury. It is essential if working with children.

And skimping on storage and closet space is false economy. Its lack not only impairs comfort, it may make efficient operation extremely difficult.

Play space that can be walled off with flexible walls may be the least expensive solution; the costly ideal might be to have a fully sealed-off playroom. And for those who work with larger groups part of the time, storage space for extra chairs, etc., is a great convenience if not a necessity.

Careful preplanning of space can help much later.

This part of setting up an office may be tedious. Who wants to get involved with all this hassle and expense? Nevertheless, this is part of what it takes to be an entrepreneur. And perhaps, "To make money, you have to spend money and time!" Entering into private practice does represent a major investment of time, energy, and money. This is true for the professions of medicine, dentistry, law, and the others. But it does have its reward both financially and in other important ways, and there is probably no job that has no tedious aspects.

Several matters should especially be attended to in reviewing the lease or other contractual agreements with the landlord, above and beyond whatever standard items are ordinarily included. One of these is the option to renew the lease with some stipulated range of costs after the original termination. The terms of most office leases range from two to five years with an option to renew, particularly if there is an extensive remodeling investment. The lease should specify provision of heating and air conditioning unless the tenant is to provide these. The same applies to regular office-cleaning services and the landlord's liability insurance for tenants and patients while in the building but outside one's office. There should be a clear statement that the tenant may place a sign on his door and on the building directory giving his name and profession (if desired). It is important to have specified the hours the building will be open and accessible to tenant and clients, and the hours that heating and/or air conditioning will be available. Many office buildings lock up at 5:30 or 6 p.m., and often turn down the heat and/or air conditioning at the same time. Also, some office buildings do not provide these services on Saturdays or Sundays, and some even turn off the regular common lighting after 6 p.m. and on weekends. Psychotherapists often see patients till relatively late in the evening and often on weekends, so obviously the timing of all these services should be clarified in advance of signing a lease. The lease should permit one to sublease to other suitable tenants like other therapists if one's personal situation demands it. Some "escape" clause should

provide for the tenant to leave the office prior to the termination of the lease, at least through his being permitted to sublease to a suitable replacement tenant.

It is money well spent to pay an attorney to review any
lease *before* it is signed. One will sleep easier, and the landlord
will respect one for taking this step. (Besides, the attorney
might well refer one or more patients later, which will more
than compensate for his fee.)

Recently many landlords have provided that their tenants
will have to pay a pro rata share of unexpected increases in
real estate taxes, and some even specify that tenants will have
to pay for unexpected increases in energy costs. One may not
be able to escape these, but at least foreknowledge will avert
unpleasant surprises later.

Furnishing an Office

Each step along the way of setting up one's office is also a
step toward commitment to private practice. Furnishing and
equipping the office is the next step in the process. To ease the
shock of the expense, it is best to shop around a bit or browse
through catalogs until it is possible to make a reasonable budget estimate. Once again, it is wise to have a relatively clear
idea of the kind of practice anticipated in order to plan the office layout. A basic guide is the simpler, the better. A second
principle: comfort over appearance, although aesthetics are
important to all of us in this sensitive business. In the 1980s,
perhaps the prototype for all psychotherapists is Judd Hirsch,
who played the psychiatrist in the movie "Ordinary People."
His office was the antithesis of Park Avenue. It had a run-
down, almost shoddy appearance. But it was comfortable for
him and for his patients, and most of all, it had the absence of

pretense which generally is the essence of all effective psychotherapies.

Because of the anxieties often associated with entering into private practice, therapists sometimes convince themselves that they must create a special environment that will foster success. In fact, the two guidelines of simplicity and comfort are paramount. The key to furnishing the office is that it be comfortable for the therapist and, to a reasonable extent, express his personality. It is true that the classical psychoanalyst would prefer his office to be anonymous, yet experience suggests that even the most austere gives himself away by his pictures of Freud or by the books on his shelf. Generally, personal family memorabilia are best kept out of the office, although most therapists enjoy having gifts from their children and family displayed in addition to diplomas, license, and professional awards. These are displayed less for patients' admiration than for the therapist's pleasure. Since the therapist's well-being is likely to make him more responsive to his patients and since he spends far more time in the office than do any patients, the office should be pleasing to him. Nevertheless, the way an office is furnished does communicate messages to patients. A child analyst whose chair was very high, while his patient's was very low, may have been wanting to impress and, indeed, dominate his patients. Some people may have been put off by the arrangement, while others may have been comforted by it. But, he furnished his office to suit his psychological tastes, and in that respect it was "right."

The taste of the therapist is clearly a determining factor in furnishing an office. Even turning the task over to an interior decorator or to an architect probably won't eliminate the therapist's imprint. It might, however, result in a generally disagreeable final product. Interior decorators and/or architects can be very helpful in selection of materials and colors. They are knowledgeable specialists in these, and they know what's available. But never must a therapist leave final decisions to them.

The basic requirements of an office are comfortable air and temperature and comfortable places to sit and to work. If the pieces of furniture come from Goodwill Industries, that will matter very little. Storage space for supplies, records, and books is a must. A secure locking filing cabinet—either two- or four-drawer—is a must. A great convenience is a small copy machine, although if a copier is readily available elsewhere, that's more efficient.

It is vital to fix a reasonable budget before making any purchases. A minimal budget of $4,000 is reasonable at the time this book is being published. Let the therapist remember, of course, that this is a capital business investment expense subject to relatively generous tax treatment.

Telephone and Answering Services

In planning the office, placement of the telephone is important, since once it's installed, the expense of moving it is high. Rates for business phones are usually higher than those for personal use. There are various special services available in some areas of the country, such as "call-forwarding," "call-waiting," and "conference calls" for relatively nominal charges. If one makes a lot of long-distance calls, there are a number of new systems that are strongly competitive with the Bell System. A few well-placed inquiries can be very useful. Generally, a simple phone hook-up with a control to turn off the bell is all that is necessary.

A telephone-answering system is a necessity. Most communities have one or more telephone-answering services where real operators answer the phone. These services vary greatly in their reliability and quality. The therapist must give very specific instructions as to how the phone is to be answered. It is best to commit these to writing. Further, he must specify what he wants the service to do with all messages. Usually, messages will be transmitted directly only to the therapist. A good answering service will probably cost about $40 per month plus installation charges. There are a variety of mechanical answering devices on the market that cost from $150 to $250. The most useful of these will give the owner the capacity to pick up messages through a remote unit that can be used at any phone. People react to these mechanical devices differently. Some resent them, some become intimidated and tongue-tied and leave garbled messages or hang up. Nevertheless, many professionals prefer the machine to a "human" answering service, since they tend to be more dependable.

Since the telephone is usually the patient's first means of contact, either directly or through the answering service or machine, it is well to consider the most pleasant and productive way to answer the phone or to have someone else answer as one's surrogate. The initial telephone call is a very important one for the patient. One patient referred to his first call as having to pick up "the 2,000-pound telephone." Generally, the basic rule in answering is to be as simple, direct, and informative as possible: "Hello, this is Dr. Doe at 342-8410." It is good to ask as few questions as possible in the initial call, and rather to express interest and arrange as early and as convenient an appointment time as possible. The answering-service person might be instructed to say, "Hello, this is the answering service for Dr. Doe, 342-8410. May I take your name and phone number and have him call you back? When would be convenient? Thank you." Or, if you plan to be away from the office for more than 24 hours, the service may be instructed to say, "Dr. Doe will not be available to return your call until _____. Is this an emergency?" If it is, arrangements ought to have been made in advance for a colleague to be available in one's absence, and the answering service should have clear instructions to contact him and to let the patient know that this is being done. If a machine is used and there is more than a 12-hour absence, it may be necessary to call in for messages regularly each day, specifying on the machine approximately when a call back may be expected. If one is unavailable because of illness, emergencies, overseas travel, or being tied up in meetings, one may need to have a colleague or a secretarial service pick up messages and return the calls with an appropriate explanation.

The message placed on a machine ought to be as simple and informative as possible: "Hello, this is Dr. Doe at 432-8410 speaking on a tape recording on my telephone-answering machine. I will be available to return your call at such and such time. In a moment you will hear a beep tone. At that sound, please tell me your name and your telephone number, and when I may conveniently telephone you. Please speak loudly and clearly. Thank you."

It is well to remember that this may be a new patient's first contact with the therapist. Rehearsing the message to be left on the tape is wise so that it is clear and the voice is steady, clear, and confident.

Announcements, Advertising, Stationery

Customarily, when a professional enters into practice, he mails out a formal announcement. This is usually done in the hope that it will generate referrals. However, experience indicates that such an announcement is the least effective source of referrals. It is better to regard the announcement as a courtesy to friends, colleagues, community "gatekeepers," and other leaders. Design of the card should be accomplished with this idea in mind. It is rarely useful to enclose a resume or a description of one's work. The rule again is the simpler, the better.

Other somewhat more effective means of advertising one's practice are listings in the yellow pages of the local telephone directories and an announcement in the local newspapers. While the several professional organizations and state licensing boards differ in their attitudes toward advertising by the members of their respective professions, a recent Supreme Court decision opened the way for advertising by all professions. There are some critics of the professions who argue strongly that each professional ought to advertise his services as part of an effort to demystify psychotherapy and to educate the consumer public about what they may expect in the way of results related to their investment of money, time, and emotional energy.

The public's interest is not likely to be served best by extensive advertising or by publishing letters of appreciation or statistics of "success" in treatment by individual therapists. Indeed, studies of "successful outcomes" of therapy are so varied as to be almost impossible for the average consumer to sort out. However, a simple statement in a newspaper announcement consisting of who the therapist is, what his credentials are, his listings in professional registries, what his experience has been, how he conducts his work, and his range of fees is not inappropriate. The statement should be straightforward, and there should be no implication that his practice is sanctioned by institutions or professional registries with which he may be associated. Honesty, as ever, in relation to all aspects of psychotherapy is the best and only acceptable policy.

The best advertisement is word of mouth from client to client or from community "gatekeepers" to potential consumers. Indeed, there is inevitably some risk to a psychotherapist in accepting "blind" referrals responding to a telephone-directory listing or a newspaper advertisement. The caller may be dangerously ill or even criminal. Some colleagues who are called by a patient who takes their name from the phone book usually suggest that the patient do at least a minimal check on them by calling the appropriate professional organization for reference in order to help the caller feel a little less at risk of having contacted a quack.

The use of advertising to build a practice continues to be distasteful to most professionals. Many would strongly agree with those who want to educate the public and demystify the practice of psychotherapy, but would choose means other than personal advertisements. Groups of professionals or professional organizations may fulfill this function best.

Usually at the time announcement cards are ordered, stationery, billing forms, and business cards are also ordered. The rule here again is to be simple and straightforward. The use of high-quality paper but simple lettering is likely to be most effective. For an extra $100 to $200 one can use a graphic artist to design a unique letterhead that can be used on stationery and billing forms, but this is more for the benefit of the therapist's ego than for the building of a practice. Many people are put off by fancy letterheads.

Usually, the return address on billing and business envelopes indicates only a suite number and address, omitting the therapist's name in the interests of the client's confidentiality. Most therapists choose to order both standard business-letter-size stationery and small personal-letter-size, in addition to billing forms. Billing forms are most conveniently designed to fit window envelopes to eliminate the work of typing name and address twice. There are also commercial record-keeping systems that automatically produce an itemized monthly bill. However, unless one's caseload is great, such systems may be superfluous.

Although many of the details of choosing one's office location and setting the office up seem mundane and even tedious, they are part of the process of making a commitment to private practice. Hopefully, this review will save new practitioners unnecessary grief and may even bring a new idea or two to more experienced people. In the next chapter, many of the practical tasks associated with an ongoing practice are enumerated and discussed.

CHAPTER 6

Practical Tasks in an Ongoing Practice

The business of business is business.

Calvin Coolidge

T HERE ARE A NUMBER of tasks associated with the reasonable running of an ongoing practice that may be accomplished with relative ease given some forethought and planning. These include the maintaining of case records, financial records, appropriate insurances, a budget, and a "business plan." Consideration of the employment of secretarial services, assistants, and consultants may also be helpful. And finally, developing a contingency plan in the event of unexpected incapacitation or death is essential.

Case Records: Purpose

The principle reasons for maintaining case records and notes in the private practice of psychotherapy are (1) to aid the therapist in understanding the patient, formulating and reformulating a treatment plan, and evaluating the accomplishments of the course of treatment; (2) as a reference or learning tool in the treatment of similar cases; (3) as a source for reporting to other professionals in the event the patient moves or the therapist must terminate, or for reporting to third-party payers, professional standard review organizations, or consultants; (4) as a source for professional writing, teaching, or consulting; (5) as a source for keeping tabs on who is making referrals; (6) as a research data source; (7) as a source for defense in case of any legal action the patient or the patient's family may take against the therapist or involving the therapist, as in divorce or child custody matters; and (8) as a means to sum up what a therapist has accomplished cumulatively over the years.

While therapists' tastes, habits, theories, practices, and preferences vary, a general rule in regard to case record keeping is to keep it as simple, brief, and concise as possible. It should fit the therapist's needs. Many therapists believe it to be pointless to attempt to keep records defensively against any possible reproach or legal attack. And unless a research design is carefully thought out in advance, voluminous case records are not likely to be useful to the private practitioner's research ambitions. Thoughtful preliminary planning about the purpose of records is essential. And a file cabinet full of records is not likely to enhance a therapist's feelings about his life's accomplishments when he's ready to retire.

When a practice matures and the therapist is fully employed by it, extensive case record keeping is likely to be a chore unless careful selectivity is exercised. There is little time for filing or retrieving useful information.

A simple approach to record keeping is the following:

Devise a form on an 8 × 11 mimeographed sheet that has space for name, age, address, home phone, work phone and place of employment, insurance coverage (name of company), spouse, age, children (names and ages), referral source, name of family doctor, date of first phone contact, date of first visit, fee amount, brief description of patient, summary of presenting problem, DSM III diagnostic designation, list of any medications patient is known to be using and other relevant data. The form might look like Figure 6.1. It is useful to get into the habit of completing this kind of form and making brief notes on each visit. For those therapists who are especially dynamically oriented, who prefer to make extensive process notes on the first few sessions or on all sessions, they can easily be attached to this face sheet. For practices that consist primarily of groups or "milieu therapy," individual face sheets like this one may need to be supplemented by some kind of group recording system that takes into account dynamic group interaction. Behavior therapists would supplement with even more detailed records or notes, as might sex therapists and "task-centered" therapists.

Generally, people in private practice tailor their recording to their own idiosyncratic needs as they perceive them. The format described above may be seen by some as too extensive, by others as too sketchy. Many practitioners have noted being struck with the realization that the most important interactions with the patient or family never get down on paper because the therapist is too busy interacting. And when notes are written after the session, they rarely seem to catch the most important dynamic points, since these often occur to the therapist a day or two later, or in the midst of someone else's session, or when he's about to fall asleep, or at some other unexpected and impossible time.

Many patients object to the therapist's maintaining any notes on them at all. Some therapists agree to destroy any that they have taken and desist from taking any more beyond those necessary for financial records. Since the Daniel Ellsberg incident during the Watergate affair in the 1970s where government officials broke into his psychotherapist's office in an attempt to find incriminating information in his case record, it has become increasingly clear that no therapist can really guarantee the confidentiality of his clients' records. Indeed, many therapists make a conscious effort, when they do take notes at all, not to include anything potentially damaging or em-

Figure 6.1   Individual Client Face Sheet

```
                                          Date_____

Name: #1_____ Age____ Home Tel.:_____

Address:_____ Work Tel.:_____

Spouse Name: #2_____ Age____ Spouse Tel.:_____
Children's Names, Ages, and Relationship (Adopted by #1 or #2):
_____

Previous Marriage(s):_____

Referral Source:_____ Fee:_____

Insurance Coverage:_____

Employer:_____

Medications Known:_____

Description of Person:_____
_____

Summary of Presenting Problem (DSM III):_____
_____

Treatment Recommendations and Goals:_____
_____

Notes: 1st Visit (Date)_____
_____

2nd Visit (Date)_____
_____

3rd Visit (Date)_____
_____

4th Visit (Date)_____
_____

Closing Summary:_____
```

barrassing to a patient—nothing about affairs, breaking the law, or others.

Nevertheless, there are developments that may push us toward more extensive record keeping. For example, peer review systems for insurance and other third-party pay systems may require detailed material to support the necessity and appropriateness of treatment. One system under consideration is reported to require a treatment report for all hospital admissions, for testing, and for psychotherapy at the eighth, twenty-fourth, fortieth, and sixtieth sessions. The reports will need to include a definition of the problem, goals of treatment, the treatment to be provided, and a description of progress. In the progress section, the patient is asked to assess whether there has been no progress, some progress, moderate progress, or goals attained. Specified goals must be concrete, related to the problem and include change expected by the next review point. Whether this system or something similar will ever be adopted by third-party payers is questionable. And, if adopted, the future findings from such a procedure are also questionable. The future of third-party payments for psychotherapists may also be questionable. There are many therapists and clients who already regard third-party payments as an intrusion into their privacy and prefer to forgo the financial aid they may bring. Obviously, most people are not so well off as to disregard them casually.

Whatever one's attitude, the matter of case record keeping will continue to be with us. Skepticism regarding the efficacy of records in portraying the reality of therapeutic encounters will continue to persist. Nevertheless, some record keeping appears to be essential and possibly useful. For example, when administering medication or collaborating with a physician who is prescribing, comprehensive record keeping is a must. An experience reported by a hypnotherapist where his patient predicted the date and time of his own death while under hypnosis is also instructive. The therapist was later shocked to learn of the patient's suicide at the precise date and time predicted while in hypnotic trance. Would careful record keeping, plus a time-tickler system, have enabled the therapist to interrupt this suicide? Perhaps not, but the possibility is too important to be dismissed out of hand.

There are several complex questions associated with case records that probably will not be readily resolved in the near future: (1) To whom do they belong, the therapist or the patient? (2) If ordered by a court, to what extent can a therapist safely resist releasing them? (3) Is there a difference between the therapist's *notes* and patient's *case record*? (4) Since confidentiality laws protect the patient rather than the therapist, can the patient demand the therapist's notes and records for his purposes even if this is to the therapist's disadvantage? Some of these questions may be resolved only through legal proceedings. In the meanwhile, they may just have to be borne by therapists even if they are disquieting.

Having thought out the purposes to which case records will be put and having devised an appropriately concise or comprehensive format, most therapists will file their records alphabetically in a locked file cabinet. Periodically, perhaps every seven years, closed files seven or more years old might be consolidated in dead storage or even destroyed.

With the availability of small computer/word processors at manageable costs, some therapists may employ them for case record storage and retrieval. A small group practice might find this time- and cost-efficient, since software packages for the special requirements of psychotherapy records may soon be available. As a research tool, and even possibly as a tool for refining diagnosis and treatment, small personal computers may soon become invaluable.

Financial Records and Computers

Computer systems are certainly effective for keeping financial records, billing, computing tax forms, reconciling checkbooks, paying bills, monitoring profit or loss, analyzing overhead costs as related to income, analyzing caseloads in relation to referral structure and location of client population, and many other uses. Most beginning practices won't generate enough work to warrant investing in a computer, although a computer can become a recreational time filler for a not fully employed therapist. For most practitioners a simple set of records is all that is necessary, and a competent accountant can help set up a format that will work. Therapists who work with a number of groups consisting of substantial numbers of individual clients may require one of the commercial record-keeping–billing systems that are readily available.

Five elements are essential in any bookkeeping system: (1) an itemized record of charges to each client, (2) an itemized record of payment by each client, (3) a summary of all receipts from client fees and practice-related income, (4) an itemized record of all practice-related expenses, and (5) a summary of all practice-related expenditures. Some simplified model forms are presented here which utilize readily available, relatively inexpensive commercial-financial record-keeping paper that is already divided into columns:

Figure 6.2   Individual Client Record Sheet

Name:_____

Address:_____   Home Phone:_____

Business Name:_____   Referred by:_____

Address:_____   Phone:_____

Insurance Co.:_____   Family Doctor:_____

Insurance Number:_____   Other Info:_____

Date of Visit	Fee	Total	Previous Balance	Payments Date/Amt.	Method of Pay:*	Balance Due: Date/Amt.

*check, cash or insurance.

Figure 6.3 Summary Sheet, Monthly, All Clients, by Office

Month: August 19____

Name (Alphabetical)	Date of Visits	Fee	Total Due for Month	Previous Balance	Payments Off. #1	Payments Off. #2	8/31/___ Bal. Due
Doe, John	10,17, 24,31	$50.00	$200.00	$150.00	$150.00		$200.00
Horn, Susan	6,13	45.00	90.00		90.00		0
May, Mary	10,17,19 24,26,31	50.00	300.00	300.00		300.00	300.00
Smart, Sam	12,19,26	50.00	150.00			150.00	0
Totals	15 visits	Avg.: $47.75	$740.00	$450.00	$240.00	$450.00	$500.00

Figure 6.4 Cash Expenses Sheet

Cash Expenses
Month of _____, 19___

Date, Description	5600 Auto Gas, Oil	5650 Auto CAB, PKG.	5330 Professional Meetings	Miscellaneous: Explanation, Amt.

Figure 6.5 All Receipts from All Sources, 19___

Page___

Date of Check	Name	Other	Client Receipts	Reimbursements	Date of Deposit	Total Deposit

Wherever possible, practice-related expenses should be paid by check through a separate business checking account, or from a single business/personal account with a number code to identify each check to determine whether it is for personal or business use. Table 6.1 is an example of a check code sheet. Each check written is coded. An accountant can put checks on a computer and provide a monthly statement organized and summarized by code. In addition, when cash expenditures are made for business purposes, a monthly summary record should be completed each month (Figure 6.4). Receipts for cash expenditures should be retained wherever possible, and/or a notation in an appointment diary for all cash expenses will simplify preparation of the monthly cash expense record and the annual tax forms.

Here is how one system may work:

1. A monthly summary sheet for all clients by office is prepared each month (Figure 6.3). All clients are listed alphabetically on this sheet. One may then dictate to a secretary or personally list day-to-day visits with each client from one's appointment diary. (Simply take each day of the month and go down appointment by appointment, noting each appointment next to the appropriate name.) All payments in cash from clients may be recorded in one's appointment diary as they are made—or may be listed in a cash receipt ledger. Once a month these may be recorded in each client's financial record sheet and also on the summary sheet. Monthly summary sheets are kept in one looseleaf binder, and individual client sheets are kept in another binder. New cases are added at the end of the summary sheet each month.

2. From the summary sheet the data are entered onto each individual client's record sheet (Figure 6.2). Each client's record sheet is filed alphabetically in a looseleaf notebook binder separately.

3. Bills for each client are prepared from his individual sheet on the last day of each month. His sheet includes each

Table 6.1: CHART OF ACCOUNTS

CODE NO.		CODE NO.	
3000	Income	8000	Personal expenses
3010	Professional fee checks	8050	Auto payments
3060	N.S.F. checks	8070	Cleaning and laundry
3980	Total income	8100	Clothing
		8120	Education
5000	Expenses	8150	Donations
5030	Associate fees	8200	Entertainment
5060	Bank charges	8300	Electric
5090	Client relations	8400	Food
5120	Depreciation	8500	Gas
5180	Insurance, general	8520	Gifts
5240	Janitorial	8550	Income tax payments
5270	Legal and audit	8600	Insurance, life
5280	Office supplies and equipment	8610	Insurance, house
5300	Outside stenographic	8630	Interest
5330	Professional dues and meetings	8650	Medical
5360	Publications, periodicals, books	8650	Hospital insurance
5390	Rent	8670	Newspapers
5420	Repairs, office	8680	Drugs
5430	Retirement fund	8700	Shelter—repairs and maintenance
5450	Stationery and postage	8750	Scavenger
5480	Taxes, other	8760	Taxes
5510	Telephone and answering service	8780	Telephone
5540	Travel	8800	House payment
5570	Unclassified	8900	House improvements
5590	Utilities	8920	Repairs
5600	Gas and oil	8930	Office loan payments
5630	Insurance, auto	8950	Vacations
5660	Licenses, auto	8960	Water
5690	Repairs, auto	8970	Unclassified
5980	Total expenses	8980	Total personal
5990	Net from practice	8990	Net

visit for the month, previous balance, payments made during the month, and the current balance as of the last day of the month (see Figure 6.2).

4. Bills are prepared to arrive on the first or second day of the following month. Figure 6.6 is a sample billing form.

5. A summary ledger sheet is kept on which are recorded all payments received by category. These are totaled for each bank deposit made, and a grand total is arrived at for each month, closing the books on the last day of the month (see Figure 6.5).

6. A summary sheet of income by month (Figure 6.7) is kept, showing numbers of interviews per month and average fee charged may then be compared by year or more often.

Figure 6.6   Sample Billing Form

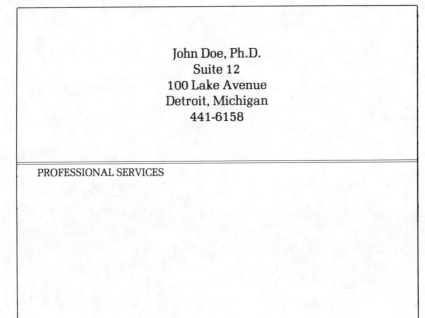

John Doe, Ph.D.
Suite 12
100 Lake Avenue
Detroit, Michigan
441-6158

PROFESSIONAL SERVICES

Figure 6.7   Summary of Income by Month

Receipts	1979	1980	1981	1982	1983
January					
February					
March					
April					
May					
June					
July					
August					
September					
October					
November					
December					
Totals					

7. A single checking account is used for both business and
personal monies, with each check coded by category (see Table
6.1, Chart of Accounts). All checks received for fees are depos-
ited in the account, and a carbon of every deposit slip listing
each client's check is kept. *It is imperative never to cash a client's check for cash, since this confuses the record keeping.* A
carbon copy of every check written is also kept—a valuable
record. The carbons are sent to an accountant, who programs
each check into a computer which sorts out business from personal and provides a monthly record by itemized categories of
both business and personal expenditures. He also reconcils
each bank statement (Figure 6.8, Coded Bank Check, and Table
6.2, Expenditures by Category). The computerized reports are
filed in looseleaf binders, and comparisons from year to year
may easily be made.

These rather complete financial records make it much
simpler to prepare income tax returns and to defend any audit.
But more important, they provide necessary data for evaluating the practice trends from year to year by month, and trends

Figure 6.8   Coded Bank Check

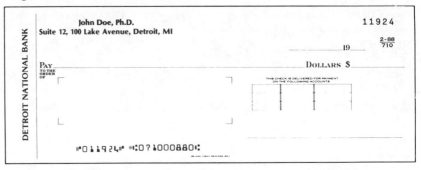

from office to office if one has more than one office. None of the data are superfluous. For example, every private practitioner experiences ups and downs in his practice. During the ups, he may wonder if he should hire an assistant or raise fees. During the downs, he may worry about how he'll pay the rent. This syndrome is common among all entrepreneurs. But trends in practice, like all other businesses, tend to by cyclical. It is useful to compare gross income by month from year to year in order to spot trends in cycles. Figure 6.7, Summary of Income by Month, permits this easily. The findings may be reassuring, or they may be a signal to make changes in one's practice organization.

Records for Third-Party Payments

Third-party payments have become increasingly frequent for all psychotherapists. Each insurance carrier tends to have its own unique claim form, although there is a tendency to make these more uniform. Blue Cross Blue Shield expects each practitioner to get a "provider number" and keep a supply of claim forms available. These can be obtained by calling the local Blue Cross administrative offices. Clients are responsible for securing appropriate claim forms for their employers. It is a

Table 6.2:   EXPENDITURES BY CATEGORY

	Current Period 9/01/80–9/30/80	Year to Date 1/01/80–9/30/80
EXPENSES, BUSINESS		
Associate Fees		$ 100.00
Bank Charges	$ 5.00	20.00
Client Relations		200.00
Depreciation	22.00	190.00
Insurance, General	457.00	3,501.12
Interest		41.00
Janitorial	90.00	270.00
Legal and Accounting	60.00	1,400.00
Office Supplies & Expense	74.75	2,240.00
Outside Stenographic	584.00	4,212.00
Professional Dues & Meetings	47.70	1,240.45
Publications, Periodicals, Books	18.90	340.00
Rent	775.00	7,900.00
Retirement Fund		7,000.00
Stationery & Postage	250.00	200.00
Taxes, Payroll	35.70	286.60
Taxes, Other	7.00	165.00
Telephone & Answering Service	390.00	3,300.00
Travel	400.00	3,400.00
Unclassified		480.00
Utilities	17.80	180.00
Gas and Oil	63.00	1,200.00
Insurance, Automobile		1,600.00
Parking and Tolls	45.00	350.00
Licenses, Automobile	30.00	140.00
Repairs, Automobile		1,500.00
Payroll Clearing Account	33.12	33.12
Total Expenses, Business	$3,405.97	$41,489.29
EXPENSES, PERSONAL		
Clothing	$ 135.00	$ 1,200.00
Education		350.00
Donations	105.00	330.00
Entertainment	84.00	1,100.00
Food	600.00	6,100.00
Furniture	80.00	80.00
Gifts	300.00	400.00
Income Tax Payments	5,100.00	21,000.00
State Income Tax Payments		1,000.00
Insurance, Life	33.33	2,700.00
Insurance, Other		600.00
Medical		1,500.00
Telephone		800.00
Unclassified		5,605.80
Total Expenses, Personal	$6,437.33	$42,765.80

desirable practice to make a clear-cut agreement with each client at the very onset of treatment that he is responsible for payment of fees, but that the therapist will cooperate by preparing the appropriate claim form so that the client may be reimbursed by the insurance company. The claim forms are generally straightforward and easily completed. Most therapists tend to be as general as possible in listing the diagnosis—for example, "depression," "anxiety reaction," "situational reaction," "bereavement reaction." In regard to "treatment," a listing of "psychotherapy (45 minutes per session)" is common. Where an insurer wants more detail, with the client's consent more may be added but, again, as little as possible. It is not always certain that the interests and purposes of insurance companies coincide with those of individual patients. The companies have at least as much obligation to prove themselves primarily concerned with the patients' best interests as do the patients and their therapists. Confidentiality is not always protected by the insurance industry. Without exception, it is wise to file a photocopy of all insurance forms completed (one more reason for having a copier easily accessible). Many find it easier to file the claim forms alphabetically together than to consolidate them with the individual patients' files, although any payments from insurance companies made directly to the therapist should be entered into the individual client's record immediately.

In summary, financial records are essential for the practitioner, for his clients, for the IRS, for the state tax agency, and for Social Security. The guiding principles for developing financial records are:

1. Think through the purpose of each record and the data needed.

2. Keep the records as simple and concise yet as complete as possible.

3. Develop simple but regular procedures for handling all checks and cash received and all monies expended, and follow

these procedures rigidly and on a strict timetable. One's appointment diary is an invaluable tool for recording any cash payments received and any cash expenses incurred (along with receipt wherever possible). When clients pay cash, it is useful to give them a simple receipt for their records and to note the payment in one's appointment diary.

4. Deposit all client fee checks in the bank. Again, *never cash a fee check for ready cash*, since that is likely to confuse record keeping. Try to pay as many practice-related expenses as possible by check, so that there is a record. Where a credit card is used for a practice-related expense, such as buying supplies or furniture or business entertaining, pay that portion of the credit card bill that is business-related with one check and the balance with a second check so that there is a convenient record through the checking account. Maintain a monthly summary sheet of all business-related cash expenses.

The illustrations in the text deserve a little extra time initially to save a great deal of time and discomfort later. Financial record keeping is basically simple but requires all the compulsivity one can bring to it. If one is lucky enough to afford a secretary or has a spouse who will do it, that may be an even happier solution.

Insurance

Peace of mind is what insurance may bring. It's a system of sharing financial risks with as many others as possible. There are at least six basic insurances a private practitioner needs to have:

1. Fire and theft

2. Physical liability coverage in case a client or other person is hurt in the office

3. Professional malpractice coverage

4. Income maintenance, at least to cover office expenses in case of disabling illness, and health insurance

5. Life insurance

6. A retirement plan—through insurance or otherwise etc.

Fire and Theft

Fire and theft insurance covers the loss of furniture and equipment in the office. While the landlord also carries site insurance, his policies will not cover tenants' possessions. Generally, this insurance is relatively reasonable. Premiums for it are tax-deductible as a business expense. Of course, if one has very little furniture or equipment or if it is all old but not yet antique and has little monetary value, one may get by without this coverage and basically be self-insured. On the other hand, in the face of inflation the replacement value of furniture and equipment may actually be increasing and one may want to increase coverage, particularly if the premium doesn't increase significantly.

Physical Liability

But no practitioner can afford to be without physical liability coverage, since accidents do happen unpredictably and without fault necessarily. Each practitioner needs at least the protection of the cost of legal fees to defend himself against suit in case of an accident, and should be protected against the possible cost of a sizable award for damages against him. Liability insurance is often sold as part of a package with fire and theft. Although the landlord also carries liability insurance, it will not protect the tenant. If the office is a part of a condominium which the therapist owns, the condo association's liability policy will usually not protect the individual owner either.

Malpractice Liability

Malpractice liability insurance is also an essential. Even if one is employed part-time in an agency or clinic that pays for malpractice coverage, that coverage often excludes private practice, so that malpractice insurance must be secured privately. Million-dollar per incident coverage is wise to purchase. Each professional association makes such insurance available to its members at advantageous group rates. But non-joiner professionals usually are able to purchase this insurance individually privately on the commercial market. One insurance company specializing in coverage for professionals is American Professional Agency, Inc., at 95 Broadway, Amityville, NY 11701. Contacting them may get you all information needed. Malpractice insurance coverage is a must even though the therapist is perfectly competent and ethical, and even though few malpractice suits are won by patients against psychiatrists, psychologists, or clinical social workers. The legal expenses for defending against such a suit even when one is fault-free are themselves enough to bring financial ruin. Even a "nuisance" suit can be costly. Table 6.3 is a summary of malpractice insurances provided by professional associations.

Some common procedures to avert potential malpractice problems include the following: *Never* release information, even on so-called "routine" forms, about a patient of any age, including children or incompetents, to anyone, including other professionals, insurance companies, credit offices, the FBI, employers, and the IRS, without a signed authorization from the patient. Whenever a patient complains and quits, or complains about a receptionist or answering service or an "unjust" bill-

Table 6.3: SUMMARY OF MALPRACTICE INSURANCES

MALPRACTICE INSURANCE FOR PSYCHOLOGISTS

LIMITS: EACH CLAIM/AGGREGATE	Annual Premium			
	Named APA Member	Unnamed Assistant	Named Non-APA Member	Unnamed Non-APA Assistant
$ 100,000/300,000	$34	$17	$ 86	$43
200,000/600,000	39	19	98	49
1,000,000/1,000,000	50	25	127	64

Rates: American Professional Agency (1983)

MALPRACTICE INSURANCE FOR SOCIAL WORKERS

LIMITS: EACH CLAIM/AGGREGATE	Annual Premium					
	NASW Member				NASW Nonmember	
	Named ACSW	Named MSW	Unnamed ACSW	Unnamed MSW	Named MSW	Unnamed MSW
$ 100,000/300,000	$33	$45	$16	$23	$ 68	$34
200,000/600,000	38	52	18	26	78	39
500,000/1,000,000	42	58	20	29	87	44
1,000,000/1,000,000	49	67	24	34	100	50

Rates: American Professional Agency (1983)

MALPRACTICE INSURANCE FOR PSYCHIATRISTS

Rates vary widely according to location of practice. Coverage is for psychiatry only—neurology and electroconvulsive therapy can increase premium by 250%.

LIMITS: EACH CLAIM AGGREGATE	Annual Premium		
	Low (Arkansas)	Medium (Idaho)	High (Calif.)
$ 100,000/300,000	$300	$550	$1,200
200,000/600,000	384	704	1,536
1,000,000/3,000,000	480	880	1,920

Rates: American Professional Agency (1983)

PROFESSIONAL LIABILITY COVERAGE FOR MENTAL HEALTH COUNSELORS

	Annual Premium				
	Marriage and Family Counselors	Licensed Mental Health Professionals	Masters Level Hypnotists or Masters in Mental Health Field	B.A. in Mental Health or School Guidance Counselors	Clergy and Pastoral Counselors
Plan 1	$ 100,000/300,000	$51	$ 74	$100	$25	$25
Plan 2	200,000/600,000	58	84	114	29	29
Plan 3	500,000/1,000,000	65	95	128	32	32
Plan 4	1,000,000/1,000,000	75	110	148	37	37

Rates: American Professional Agency (1983)

Source: American Professional Agency, Inc., 95 Broadway, Amityville, NY 11701. Used by permission.

ing, the therapist should talk with the patient directly and attempt to resolve the problem. Frequently, where a dependent is in treatment that is paid for by another, there are dynamic issues that may be acted out through dissatisfaction with billing or rage at a receptionist or at the therapist. Sometimes these are feelings displaced from others, but they may result in a malpractice suit. For example, a therapist recently began bill collection proceedings against the divorced father of a teenage patient who lived with her mother. In response, the father initiated a "nuisance" malpractice suit against the therapist, ultimately offering to drop the malpractice suit if the therapist dropped the bill collection. In this instance, the therapist decided to accept the offer because it would have cost him so much time in giving depositions, etc., that the benefits would have been outweighed. To avoid such situations, it is wise to prevent the build-up of back fees even if treatment must be interrupted, except by specific, possibly even written agreement, with the person responsible for paying the bill. In cases of divorce and treatment of dependents, this is especially wise.

In addition, each therapist who employs a secretary, another therapist, or even an answering service is responsible for their actions. Therefore, one must take responsibility for training them adequately and clearly and making sure they know what is expected of them. For example, a secretary must never discuss one patient with another, even to the extent of naming the patient, an often overlooked detail. And no one ought to be given any kind of drug, even an aspirin, by a therapist's secretary or by any therapist who does not have a medical license.

Income Maintenance Insurance and Major Medical Insurance

Income maintenance insurance, health insurance, and life insurance may be considered optional by some, but most practitioners regard them as essential. If one is employed full- or part-time, health insurance coverage through the employment group is probably cheaper than anything that can be purchased privately. Often major medical insurance with a $500 deductible provision and coverage up to $1,000,000 in a lifetime can be secured at reasonable rates through small groups assembled for this purpose. The Phoenix Mutual Life Insurance Company, Hartford, Connecticut, tends to write this kind of insurance for small groups of professionals, but sells it as part of a package that includes life insurance and income maintenance insurance. Marsh and McLennan Group Associates, New York, offers a similar package at competitive rates.

The respective professional associations usually sell group packages of income maintenance, major medical, and life at favorable rates. However, in at least one instance (NASW), the lifetime limits of the major medical policy are only $50,000, which may be inadequate protection. One-million-dollar lifetime coverage is more realistic. Premiums for income maintenance insurance that is designed to cover the ongoing expenses of office operations—rent, telephone, answering service, secretarial, insurances, etc.—in case of disabling illness may be considered a tax-deductible business expenses. Special policies for this purpose are offered by the American Psychological Association and the American Psychiatric Association. If one is incorporated, all health insurance premiums, most medical bills, and some life insurance premiums may under certain circumstances be deducted as business expenses. Table 6.4 is a summary of income maintenance insurances offered through the professional associations. See also Table 6.5.

The American Psychiatric Association and the American Psychological Association also offer "Professional Overhead Expense Insurance," to meet the cost of maintaining an office and other professional and business expenses during total disability. The benefits may range from $300 to $3500/month. For psychiatrists aged 50–59, $1000/monthly benefit costs $165/year. For psychologists 50–54 it's $146/year; for 55–59 it's $196/year.

Table 6.4:   INCOME MAINTENANCE INSURANCE OFFERED THROUGH PROFESSIONAL ASSOCIATIONS

AMERICAN PSYCHOLOGICAL ASSOCIATION
(Liberty Mutual Insurance Company)

Benefits are paid for a maximum of 10 years but at a decreasing rate: 100% for 2 years, 75% for 1 year, 50% for 1 year, 33⅓% for 3 years, 25% for 3 years.

DAY BENEFITS START	Annual Premium for $100 Weekly Benefit at Ages—				
	35–39	40–44	45–49	50–54	55–59
29	$57	$80	$106	$160	$214
91	36	51	68	103	138
366	20	28	37	56	76

American Psychological Group Insurance Plan.

NATIONAL ASSOCIATION OF SOCIAL WORKERS

Plan 1: Benefits for a maximum of 5 years if disabled by accident, for a maximum of 2 years if disabled by illness (but not past 65).

DAY BENEFITS START	Annual Premium for $1,000 Monthly Benefit at Ages—				
	18–29	30–39	40–49	50–59	60–64
15	$130	$160	$194	$284	$416

Plan 2: Benefits until age 65 if disabled by accident, for a maximum of 5 years if disabled by illness (but not past 65).

DAY BENEFITS START	Annual Premium for $1,000 Monthly Benefit at Ages—				
	18–29	30–39	40–49	50–59	60–64
15	$150	$199	$254	$414	$532
91	84	114	166	298	382

National Association of Social Workers Insurance Trust Plan.

AMERICAN PSYCHIATRIC ASSOCIATION

Benefits for life if disability starts before age 50; to age 65 if disability starts between age 50 and age 64; for 1 year if disability starts between age 64 and age 70.

DAY BENEFITS START	Annual Premium for $1,000 Monthly Benefit at Ages—				
	35	35–39	40–44	45–49	50–69
1	$220	$280	$360	$420	$470
31	170	210	260	370	400
181	120	140	170	280	300

American Psychiatric Association Plan.

Sources: Data selected from Plans' advertising materials.

Table 6.5: DISABILITY BENEFITS

INDIVIDUAL DISABILITY INSURANCE

When an individual disability plan is bought, the premium is set when the policy is issued and doesn't increase with age. The premium figures shown below are typical of many insurace companies. They provide benefits that will be paid to age 65. For additional premiums, extra features may be added. There are plans, for example, that provide partial payments when back at work but not earning full income. Other plans keep paying off if one can't resume previous activities—even if one is able to work at a different type of job.

DAY BENEFITS START	Premium for $1,000 Monthly Benefit at Age—					
	30	35	40	45	50	55
15	$450	$540	$650	$785	$940	$1,080
31	400	480	580	700	850	990
61	350	425	515	625	740	875
91	325	390	475	575	690	790
181	290	350	425	500	625	700

DISABILITY BENEFITS FROM SOCIAL SECURITY

Benefits from Social Security go into effect when one has been disabled for 5 months—if the disability is expected to last a year or more. They will be adjusted regularly for inflation, so these current figures give a good idea of the level of help one can expect. From age 50 to age 62 the benefit remains fairly constant; after age 62 retirement benefit rates apply. Benefits are estimates for those who have made maximum Social Security contributions.

YOUR AGE NOW	Monthly Benefits		
	No Dependents	One Dependent	Maximum
30	$612	$918	$1,070
35	543	814	949
40	499	749	874
45	465	697	813
50	443	665	776

Source: "Tax and Financial Planner," *Psychotherapy Finances*, 1978, p. 35. (Permission of publisher applies to Table 6.6 also.)

Life Insurance

As an independent entrepreneur each of us needs to consider our own insurance needs, since no employer will do it for us. There are commercial guides available to assist in computing need. The Consumer's Union has published comprehensive data on this matter, as has *Psychotherapy Finances*: "Tax and Financial Planner," 1978. The professional associations sell term life insurance at favorable rates. Table 6.6 excerpted from *Psychotherapy Finances*, summarizes the rates. According to many advisers, term life insurance policies tend to offer the most economical coverage, although they accumulate no cash surrender value. Rates and terms vary widely, and it is wise to shop for the best ones.

Retirement

Many advisers suggest that insurance annuity programs for retirement are often not the best vehicles. Keogh Plans enable the self-employed to put away as much as 15 percent of their earned income tax-free for retirement, and in addition, one does not have to pay taxes on income earned on monies in the fund until one begins withdrawing income upon his retirement. This is likely to be a superior mechanism to accumulate retirement funds.

Social Security

As a self-employed person, you are required to pay Social Security taxes on income earned unless you are employed else-

Table 6.6: TERM LIFE INSURANCE FROM PROFESSIONAL ASSOCIATIONS

For straight term insurance, one is not likely to find rates lower than those offered in an associations' group policy. The American Psychological Association policy includes double indemnity for accidental death and full payment for dismemberment—psychiatrists can add these features for $1 per $1,000, social workers for $.72 per $1,000. Rates are for the maximum amounts offered, with some adjustments to make the different policies comparable.

ANNUAL PREMIUM COST PER $1,000 BY AGE	*American Psychological Association*	*National Association of Social Workers*	*American Psychiatric Association*
Under 30	$ 2.10	$ 1.70	$ 2.60
30–34	2.45	1.83	3.02
35–39	3.24	2.36	3.88
40–44	4.72	3.49	5.70
45–49	7.26	5.32	8.78
50–54	11.20	8.28	13.66
55–59	17.23	12.84	20.98
Maximum Available	$80,000	$75,000	$100,000

Source: "Tax and Financial Planner," *Psychotherapy Finances*, 1978, p. 35.

where and your Social Security payments there reach the maximum required by law. Of course, Social Security insurance does represent a basic retirement floor for most professionals, but it usually must be supplemented by plans like those indicated above.

Workmen's Compensation Insurance and Unemployment Compensation

Finally, one may be required by law to purchase workmen's compensation insurance and pay state and federal premiums for unemployment compensation if one employs any staff, like a secretary or other assistants or if one is incorporated and is legally an employee. An accountant should advise on all of these matters, but the more the professional knows about them himself, the better served he will be.

To summarize briefly, this section has reviewed the basic insurances a private practitioner must have, including physical liability (sometimes included with malpractice liability); fire and theft; malpractice liability for one's self and for one's professional employees; major medical insurance; income maintenance insurance; life insurance; Social Security, workmen's compensation, and unemployment insurances; and retirement plans. Shopping around for the best plans at the best prices available is recommended.

Secretary

The advantages of having one's own secretary are self-evident. Many therapists find that they cannot function efficiently without a secretary who is an extra right arm, doing bills, paying bills, bookkeeping, filing, taking dictation, and generally helping to organize and administrate their professional lives. Unfortunately, few psychotherapists generate enough secretarial work to warrant employing a person even half-time although most could use a person for about one-fifth time. There are two options available to most: (1) to use a secretarial service on an as-needed basis; (2) to employ a secretary together with one or more professionals (not necessarily therapists) who are physically located very close by. The latter of these options is likely to be preferable and even less expensive. The first option makes for difficulties with confidentiality, rigidity, and quality control and is usually more expensive. In going into an arrangement to participate with other professionals in employing a secretary, it is essential to commit whatever is agreed upon to writing, including available hours, responsibilities for supervision, and costs (including overhead, equipment, supplies, salary, and taxes and benefits). Often it is convenient to contract with another professional who employs a secretary for a set minimum number of hours of work for a set fee, with

additional hours charged for separately. Hourly pay for a secretary ranges from $4.50 to $10 depending on skills, experience, location, full-time versus part-time, and availability in the
market.

When one employs a secretary, the hiring process is crucial, as are certain ongoing procedural basics. First and fore-
most, one should only hire a secretary whom one likes. The relationship between a secretary and a therapist is crucial to his
practice and how it is conducted. Usually, the secretary is the
first to have contact with new patients. How he presents himself to the patients will affect how the patient initially perceives the therapist. To a large extent the secretary is regarded as the therapist's alter ego by patients, and in fact he is.
Discretion, good humor, patience, empathy, directness, and
honesty are all requirements above and beyond intelligence, efficient technical skill, accuracy, and a good mind for organizing
things. When a therapist is fortunate enough to find such a person, he should be careful to assess the secretary's needs for financial progress, fringe benefits, time flexibility, and career
progression. Salary should be reviewed at least every six
months or more frequently. (The secretary should be instructed
to remind his employer of time for review.) Signs of discomfort
or displeasure should be responded to immediately.

In the hiring process, one should defer employing someone
until adequately assured of a good match. Personality characteristics and intelligence are likely to be more important than
clerical skills. A combination of both is rare and, when discovered, must be cherished and nourished.

Professional Assistants

As a practice grows, one may reach a point where there
appears to be a need to employ one or more assistants. For example, many family therapists prefer to have a co-therapist of

the opposite sex available for all or many of their cases. Child therapists may want to have less than fully trained or recently graduated assistants available sometimes for work with especially disturbed or acting-out children in the child's own home, or even in the therapist's home—especially therapists who are dedicated to milieu therapy. Group therapists also often require the help of assistants, and therapists who use video tapes of sessions as a therapeutic tool may employ professional assistants.

In all instances, arrangements should be described in writing for the protection of both the therapist and the assistant. Payment may be hourly or by fixed salary. In every instance it is vital that malpractice insurance specifically covering the assistant be secured.

It sometimes happens that a therapist employs an assistant with the express idea held by both that the assistant will ultimately move into private practice himself, or into a partnership or other similar arrangement. A written agreement or contract that specifies the time frame within which the assistant may expect to move from "assistant" status to fully equal partner or independent practitioner will minimize many serious psychological or status conflicts and financial disputes that can sour otherwise useful collaborations. The importance of the process of arriving at a written agreement satisfactory to all parties at the onset of a working relationship cannot be emphasized enough.

An example is the following: A therapist employs an assistant whom he agrees to pay for consultations with patients whom he will refer. He agrees to the assistant's receiving an increasing portion of the gross fee computed to reflect the increasing proportion of overhead expenses the assistant will meet as the volume of his appointments increases. The agreement is consolidated in writing. The contract stipulates payment to the assistant only after the patient has paid his fee.

In arrangements observed indirectly through treatment of other professionals like doctors, dentists, and lawyers, some of us have come to realize that clear-cut agreements, with certain escape clauses for both parties, are essential for the preservation of good working relationships between assistants and employers. Many therapists believe that professionals who sign on as an assistant ought to insist on a regular progression to full partnership status or to full status as an equal colleague in a private practice, or to equal or pro rata ownership in a professional corporation. This encourages professional and personal growth for the professional assistant, and minimizes the temptation toward exploitation of the assistant financially or psychologically by the senior practitioner(s). This may not be the ordinary pattern in law partnerships, or possibly in medical partnerships. It may be that the consequences of the standard procedures in law partnerships work to the disadvantage of consumers and do not lead to the optimum professional growth of the apprentice-assistants. It is possible that this manner of organizing practices has a tendency to inflate costs to the consumer—in a way that is similar to the fee-splitting customs ethically forbidden to physicians. Certainly, in the practice of psychotherapy much depends for its success, as perceived by the patient, on the clear responsibility of individual therapist to patient. Attempts to substitute one therapist for another are fraught with a great burden of psychological tearing, so that corporate-type practice is likely to be detrimental to patient and therapist and is likely to have a subtle or not so subtle inflationary impact on fees not dissimilar to fee splitting. It seems highly desirable that there be agreement leading to full participation in the practice by professional assistants within a reasonable period of time. If an assistant is found to be less than fully competent in the judgment of his employer(s), that should be determined within a 6- to 12-month period—no more. In that instance, the assistant should be relieved of responsibility, and, with appropriate responsibility assumed for his patients on an individualized basis, he should be asked to leave. In all other instances, the assistant should move relatively quickly, within three to five years, to full participation. Again, if the assistant and/or employer(s) should find themselves at odds with each other or there should be any instance of clear negligence, they should feel free to terminate their relationship. The assistant's patients should be free to choose to continue with him or to choose another therapist. In no way, after 12 months, should any assistant regard his patients as "owned" by his employer(s). And even before then, of course, patients have the right to choose their therapists. This is the essence of private practice from the consumer's point of view—the right to choose—particularly after he has the opportunity to be informed and to make an informed choice.

There may be some rationale in other kinds of practices, like medical or dental or legal, for one professional to employ another with indefinite status as an employee. Yet observation suggests that this eventually leads to serious conflict, dissolution of the arrangement, sometimes corrupt and even criminal behaviors, and frequently lawsuits between professionals. Inevitably, the consumer suffers. On principle, many psychotherapists disapprove such an arrangement.

In summary, assistants may be vital to the conduct of certain kinds of therapies like family or group therapy, or when a practice expands to the point where no one therapist can reasonably manage it. Employing assistants is an excellent way for more experienced therapists to train the less experienced and to expand a practice to the consumer's advantage. It is also an excellent way for an assistant to enter private practice in stages with minimal capital expenditures, and for experienced therapists to gratify their "mentoring" needs while protecting their own practices and referral sources. But in any such arrangement, a clearly written agreement specifying a probationary period of no more than 12 months and leading within a specified time frame lasting no longer than five years to full and equal participation of the assistant is essential. In any instance, no patient shall be considered to be "owned" by the employer, since in private practice it is essential to guard the patient's right to choose therapists. Indeed, this right should be guaranteed to all patients in non-private practice settings as well.

Consultants

Consultants serve a very different purpose from assistants or supervisors. Both medical psychotherapists and nonmedical therapists may employ them. It is essential to understand that a consultant does not take responsibility for the treatment of a patient. His role is to consult with the primary therapist, who is solely responsible for the treatment of the patient. Essentially the consultant is a teacher, or someone who brings special expertise by virtue of his specialization to a consultee who is not as conversant with the special area in which the consultant is knowledgeable. The role of a consultant is clearly differentiated from the role of a supervisor, who may indeed maintain responsibility for the patient through the direct therapist. A therapist in private practice is responsible for his patient, although in the instance of a less experienced assistant, the assistant as an employee may be delegated responsibility for the treatment of a patient under the careful supervision of his employer. But a consultant never assumes responsibility for the treatment. When that occurs, he is no longer a consultant, but a supervisor. In some instances, a consultant may be a psychopharmacologist who prescribes medication for a patient who is in psychotherapy with another therapist, who may be a physician or a nonphysician. In such a situation, the psychopharmacologist assumes direct responsibility for prescribing the medication, and in that respect is no longer functioning altogether as a consultant, but as a collaborating therapist. He may function as a consultant to the primary psychotherapist in teaching about expected behaviors associated with the medication and in relation to effects to be watched for and other procedures to be followed. In some instances where medications are prescribed by a psychopharmacologist, it may be appropriate for a clear-cut agreement to be made between psychotherapist, patient, and psychopharmacologist that the latter is assuming primary responsibility for the patient's treatment. Generally, when a significant treatment relationship between psychotherapist and patient has been established and the psychopharmacologist's help is sought, the psychotherapist is likely to be preferable as the primary therapist.

Nonmedical therapists especially, but medical therapists too, often will seek consultation from medical specialists like internists, neurologists, urologists, and oncologists, but they will retain primary responsibility for the psychotherapy. Or a therapist who runs into problems with special kinds of treatment modalities with which he is not completely confident, like family or sex therapy, may call upon a specialist for consultation and advice, retaining primary responsibility for the psychotherapy. Or when a therapist suspects he has some countertransference problems with a particular patient, he may seek consultation.

As a general rule, neither a consultant nor a supervisor should also attempt to enter into a psychotherapeutic treatment relationship with the consultee or supervisee. Nor should a consultee or a supervisee attempt to enlist the aid of his own psychotherapist as a case consultant. The reason is that too many extraneous issues come to surround, or are introduced into, the patient's treatment situation, usually without the patient's knowledge or consent, and they may tend to confound the treatment process.

No therapist, no matter how competent or experienced, is above needing consultation from time to time. Admittedly, it is somewhat more difficult because of extraneous psychological issues for an older, experienced therapist to seek consultation, especially from a younger colleague. Yet in this complex field there is no shame in seeking consultation at any time. One experienced therapist recalled his outrage when a member of his own family had been in treatment with a prominent, experienced, well-thought-of psychoanalyst for some time and the analyst decided treatment was at a standstill. The analyst's only suggestion was that the patient undergo a battery of projective tests to determine his dynamic problems. It was observed that if treatment was at a standstill, the therapist ought first to seek consultation for himself, preferably from another experienced psychoanalyst. This suggestion that the patient get projective testing appeared to be the analyst's cop-out because, first, he wouldn't have to expose himself to the psychologist or another consultant, and second, the psychologist performing the projective tests would have lesser status and therefore present less threat. But the patient, after a major investment of time, energy, and money, might have been better served had the analyst been confident enough, big enough, and wise enough to seek consultation and perhaps gain new perspective and possibly take a different, more productive tack. Projective tests may be useful during the course of treatment. But they ought never be used as a dodge from responsibility. In this instance, the recommendation seemed to be an example of an ancient technique: if treatment fails, blame the patient. A strong, competent, knowledgeable, tactful, and skillful consultant may be useful to any therapist at any stage of professional experience and development.

The Nonmedical Practitioner and Consultants

Nonmedical psychotherapists often turn to medical psychiatrists, especially psychoanalysts, for consultation. They tend to do this more frequently early in their practice. Such consultation may be helpful, but some have observed that it often is essentially a hand-holding, reassuring process. Consultation generally is most useful when it has some specified purpose. For example, when a therapist, medical or nonmedical, is treating a dangerously suicidal or homicidal patient, consultation is most useful. Nonmedical therapists who want to establish relationships with a medical psychiatrist so that they will have back-up in case they need to hospitalize a patient will sometimes arrange for regular consultation with such a person as a kind of insurance of his availability in an emergency. Perhaps this is sometimes necessary, but it seems a poor reason to seek consultation. Back-up physicians for hospitalization, medication, or other similar purposes can be arranged in advance for these specific purposes. Genuine consultation should serve more genuine, forthright purposes.

In summary, consultation may be vital to any psychotherapist, but its function should be clearly distinguished from that of supervisor. Consultants generally do not carry primary responsibility for a patient's treatment. Consultation usually is for special educational purposes, including dealing with countertransference problems. Usually one's own therapist ought not to function as one's case consultant. And back-up physicians who may medicate or hospitalize in an emergency ought to be sought out in advance for this specific purpose, not employed under the guise of consultant where the back-up is the only purpose of the consultation.

Incorporation

Opinion is divided on the question of whether a solo practitoner or a group of practitioners ought to incorporate. There is general agreement that the single most important possible advantage of incorporating is the opportunity to develop a tax-sheltered retirement plan. That is, where one is incorporated, one can put more than $15,000 a year into a retirement plan that is tax-sheltered. As an unincorporated solo practitioner one is limited to 15 percent of net practice income before taxes up to $15,000 a year (excluding all other income such as spouse's salary) that can be put into a tax-sheltered Keogh Fund in addition to an IRA account. In either instance, earnings on these funds are not taxed, but the funds are unavailable to one until age 59 or older. Obviously, if one does not have enough surplus income to put into the retirement fund, this feature is not of much use.

Incorporation does, however, enable one to pay certain fringe benefits out of *pretax dollars*. These may include (1) premiums on up to $50,000 of term life insurance, and (2) 100 percent of medical, dental, and disability costs, either by buying insurance or by direct reimbursement (ordinarily if not incorporated, only those costs exceeding 3 percent of gross income may be deducted for tax purposes).

A possible one-time *deferral* of a proportion of one year's income taxes may be achieved by incorporating in July with a January 31 end-of-fiscal-year date. If one can forgo drawing salary from the corporation for the last six months of a tax year (July 1 to December 31), then be paid a bonus in the next taxable year (after January 1), a proportion of the current year's taxes may be deferred to some year in the future. The catch is the need to have enough savings or borrowing capacity to provide personal living-expense money for the six-month period. The idea is that one's personal taxable income will be reduced by half for one year, as will the corporation's tax liability. There is a possibility that the IRS may question the procedure. Eventually, of course, a tax will be paid, but one has the use of the deferred tax dollars for investment, etc., for an indefinite number of years.

Other advantages of incorporating that are sometimes cited are purchase and maintenance of an auto by the corporation. However, use of the auto for personal purposes is taxable on personal income tax as income "in kind," so that there is little actual tax saving to be realized that would not be available to an unincorporated practitioner.

Some of the disadvantages of incorporating are extra costs for Social Security taxes, state and federal unemployment taxes, workman's compensation tax, additional annual costs for filing reports to the state's secretary of state, separate accounting, additional federal and state corporate income tax filings, a separate set of books for the corporation, and a separate checking account. Legal costs for forming a corporation will be in the $2,000 to $3,000 range. If one chooses to adopt a "defined benefit retirement" program, there will be actuarial costs of $1,000 to $3,000 in order for the program to meet the IRS requirements. In addition, certain minimum contributions annually may be mandatory.

If one has employees, any pension or other benefits adopted by the corporation must be available to them on a non-discriminatory basis if they are employed more than half-time.

If the corporation includes more than one practitioner, the special individual needs of each become a problem in designing a benefit package. For example, if one practitioner is 55 to 60 and another is 30 to 35, their pension needs are likely to differ markedly.

Not all states permit incorporation of stockholders from different professions such as psychiatrists, psychologists, and clinical social workers. Not all states permit social workers or psychologists to form professional corporations, but some of those that don't permit this do permit formation of another type of corporation. Legal consultation obviously is necessary to clarify such matters.

Summarizing, the major advantage of incorporating is to permit developing a larger tax-sheltered retirement program than one can develop unincorporated. There are significant complications and disadvantages to incorporating. A practitioner with net *practice* income (excluding any other income) of more than $75,000 per year may consider incorporating advantageous. Incorporating appears to be only marginally advantageous to those whose net practice income is much less.

Discussion with a competent accountant and a tax lawyer may help one come to a decision on the issue. One caveat here. Some insurance salespeople, "estate planners," or "investment counselors" may offer to do an evaluation and set up retirement or investment programs and incorporate one at little or no cost. However, they may have their own agenda, which may include selling their company's insurance package. It is wiser to invest in an independent evaluation, asking the accountant and lawyer to give an estimate of their fees in advance.

Annual Budget

All professionals in private practice need to view their practice in some respects as a business. One way to begin to organize one's practice in a businesslike way is to develop an annual budget relating expenses to income and calculating annual "profit." This will also certainly help one to calculate deductible expenses for tax purposes. See Table 6.7 for such a budget. It includes the major budget items, estimated income for a full-time practice, and estimated net income or profit. Since costs vary from one geographical location to another, and how one desires to conduct one's practice will vary individually, specific dollar amounts are presented here only as rough estimates. Each practitioner must perform his own calculations.

The net profit estimate in Table 6.7 may be high or low. Variation in gross income obviously can be great. For example, if the average fee is $45 times 38 visits times 4.3 weeks per month times 10.5 months, annual gross drops to $77,000—or to

Table 6.7: BUDGET FOR A FULL-TIME PRACTICE

ITEMS	Expenses		Income		Net Profit Before Taxes	
	Monthly	Annually	Monthly	Annually	Monthly	Annually
Rent	$ 400	$ 4,800				
Office Cleaning	30	360				
Utilities	20	240				
Telephone	150	1,800				
Answering Service	50	600				
Secretarial[1]	100	1,200				
Other Services	50	600				
Supplies	20	240				
Postage	20	240				
Equip. Maintenance[2]	100	1,200				
Prof. Travel	100	1,200				
Insurance:						
Office Liability	17	204				
Prof. Liability	10	120				
Income Protection[3]	50	600				
Health (Major Medical)	100	1,200	40 visits/week @ $45 = $1,800 × 45 weeks = $81,000			

Fire & Theft	10	120
Life	50	600
Unemp. Compensation	10	120
W'kmen's Compensation	10	120
Auto	100	1,200
Social Security	120	1,500
Consultants & Cont. Ed.	100	1,200
Prof. Organizations	30	360
Prof. Meetings	25	300
Periodicals/Literature	40	480
Legal/Accounting Fees	85	1,000
Retirement[4]	(625)	(7,500)
Totals	$1,795	$21,600	$6,750[5]	$81,000	$4,9555	$59,460

[1]Minimum estimate.

[2]Amortized over 5–10 years.

[3]This amount provides only for maintaining one's office during an illness. For personal expenses, additional income maintenance insurance should be purchased.

[4]Up to $15,000/year, or 15% of net profit from practice excluding all other income (e.g., spouse's salary or investment income). Average $7,500. Not included in totals.

[5]The montly income is distributed over 12 months. However 10.5 months/year is actually spent working. Vacations, holidays, and meetings account for the remaining time not spent working.

$75,000 at 10 months per year. Or if 20 visits per week at $45 per visit = $900 times 44 weeks, the gross is only $40,000 per year. Obviously, production, size of fee and its collection, and control of costs are the three vital elements in determining profitability and provide the necessary comparison with other means of earning a living upon which reasonable career decisions may be based.

Most management consultants would recommend that private practitioners develop a "business plan." Most simply described, this is an estimate of expenses projected monthly over a time span, usually a year or longer, compared to estimated income. It may include a cash flow chart. Table 6.8 is a simple example of such a chart.

Assumptions underlying the projections of Table 6.8 are:

1. Expenses are computed for a full-time, solo practice in line with the sample budget shown in Table 6.7 excluding expenses for secretary, travel, life insurance and "other services" for the first two years.

2. Income projections are based on the following:
   a. Fee is: $45 per visit; it is multiplied by number of-visits.
   b. Estimated number of visits begins with 10 per week times 4 = 40 per month, with 5 percent increase in visits each month for 2½ years.
   c. Monies actually received are 50 percent at the time of each visit. Remaining balance of 50 percent is collected within 60 days.

3. To develop your own cash flow chart, use the fee you expect to collect and your estimate of growth of practice and proportion of fees collectible at time of visit. Fee times visits per month times 50 percent = monthly income plus receivable proportion of previous month's billed fees = actual monthly income less your estimated expenses = net profit.

Table 6.8   SAMPLE CASH FLOW CHART

	Annual Totals	Jan.	Feb.	Mar.	Apr.	May	June	July	Aug.	Sept.	Oct.	Nov.	Dec.
FIRST YEAR													
No. of visits	634	40	42	44	46	48	51	53	56	59	62	65	68
Actual Receipts (Est.)	$26,407	900	1,800	1,890	1,980	2,070	2,182	2,283	2,401	2,527	2,658	2,790	2,925
Receivables	1,530	900	945	990	1,035	1,080	1,147	1,192	1,260	1,327	1,395	1,462	1,530
Expenses	17,940	1,495	1,495	1,495	1,495	1,495	1,495	1,495	1,495	1,495	1,495	1,495	1,495
Net Profit (Loss)	$8,469	(595)	305	395	485	575	687	788	906	1,032	1,163	1,296	1,430
SECOND YEAR													
No. of visits	1,129	71	74	78	82	86	91	95	100	105	110	116	121
Actual Receipts	$48,835	3059	3,195	3,510	3,600	3,735	3,915	4,095	4,297	4,510	4,730	4,975	5,209
Receivables	2,722	1,597	1,665	1,755	1,845	1,935	2,047	2,137	2,250	2,362	2,475	2,670	2,722
Expenses	17,940	1,495	1,495	1,495	1,495	1,495	1,495	1,495	1,495	1,495	1,495	1,495	1,495
Net Profit	$30,891	1,564	1,700	2,015	2,105	2,240	2,420	2,600	2,802	3,015	3,235	3,480	3,715
THIRD YEAR													
No. of Visits	1,808	127	133	140	147	154	162	170	175	175	175	175	175
Actual Receipts	$88,486	5,580	5,850	6,142	6,458	6,772	6,952	7,470	7,762	7,875	7,875	7,875	7,875
Receivables	3,937	2,857	2,992	3,150	3,307	3,465	3,645	3,825	3,937	3,937	3,937	3,937	3,937
Expenses	18,120	1,510	1,510	1,510	1,510	1,510	1,510	1,510	1,510	1,510	1,510	1,510	1,510
Net Profit	$66,479	4,070	4,340	4,630	4,950	5,262	5,442	5,960	6,365	6,365	6,365	6,365	6,365

131

A "business plan" based on these kinds of projections would suggest (1) how much money in savings or loans would be required to sustain a practitioner through the first years of practice; (2) how many referrals would be needed to attain the projected interview count; (3) whether or not to maintain a full-time or part-time job while the practice is building; (4) whether to sublet space and equipment from someone else while the practice is building or whether to take an office, equip it, and sublet it to another person in order to reduce overhead.

All of these considerations and decisions would ultimately lead to developing a business plan which would offer a means of measuring progress, provide a frame work within which one could function with some security, and provide a base from which to make other decisions.

Contingency Plan In Case of Incapacitation or Death

Finally, anyone in private practice has the obligation to have a formal, or at least an informal, understanding with at least one other professional for the management of his practice in case of an emergency or even death. Usually, a simple arrangement is all that is necessary—yet it is vitally important to patients at such a critical time to know that their therapist cared enough to have thought about them in advance. A colleague needs to have access to the therapist's records of names, addresses, and phone numbers of his patients and, if possible, his appointment diary. Naturally, if one has a full- or part-time secretary or someone who does the billing, the mechanics are simplified.

The colleague needs to be instructed in advance to phone each patient personally and inform him of what has happened simply, answering questions as directly as possible though not volunteering more than the client seeks, especially in case of a death. An offer to see the patient as quickly as possible, or to arrange for him to be seen by another therapist as quickly as possible, is essential. In the instances of death or other calamitous events, it is best to be somewhat directive with the patient, encouraging him to talk with a therapist immediately. Whether or not the back-up therapist will charge for this service is an open question. Perhaps a single visit should not be charged for, but subsequent visits would require a fee to be negotiated, not necessarily the same fee charged by the deceased or otherwise incapacitated therapist. Any fees owed to the therapist should be collected as quickly as possible and, in the case of death, included in his estate. This is important both financially and psychologically to help the patient effect closure and enter into the bereavement and mourning process. For therapist-colleagues who agree to undertake this mournful task, it is not inappropriate to share feelings of mourning with the bereaved patients. In the instance of a crisis other than death, judgment based on actual assessment of the realities will determine what information is best shared with clients, and what withheld. Some examples of difficult judgment situations are: a therapist's attempted suicide; mental breakdown; acute physical illness, especially one that may be terminal; a crisis in the therapist's personal life that immobilizes him and others. There are no prescribed procedures to follow at such times, though the guiding principle ought to be whatever appears to be dynamically in the client's best interest at the particular time, with the interest of the afflicted therapist of only secondary importance.

Another issue that is difficult and complicated for a therapist, client, colleague, profession, and community is the instance of a therapist who becomes addicted to alcohol or other drugs. Even for the therapist who has made appropriate arrangements with a colleague for unexpected emergencies, few are prepared for this. Recently, some professionals have established hot-lines to help fellow professionals. However, these efforts sometimes fall short in helping colleagues. Again, the interests of clients must take precedence in determining the interventions of professionals vis-à-vis other professionals. For further information one may contact: Psychologists Helping Psychologists, (313) 565-3821; or Social Workers Helping Social Workers, (203) 566-2696; or write: New York Chapter of NASW, 79 Madison Avenue, New York, New York, 10016, for the pamphlet, *Alcoholism Among Social Workers: Approaching a Colleague with a Drinking Problem*; or contact Dr. Richard Kilburg, (202) 833-7600.

Selling or Buying a Practice

An alternative to dying in one's practice "with one's boots on" is to sell it. An alternative to beginning one's practice from scratch is to buy into an existing one. The advantages are obvious for the seller:

1. He offers a relatively well-controlled resource to his patients and referral sources.

2. He is permitted some evaluation of a successor, and this provides some protection for his patients.

3. He realizes some financial reward from a lifelong practice-building effort.

For the buyer the advantages are equally obvious:

1. He gets a built-up practice and office.

2. The practice may come with a built-in mentor.

Referral sources are the most valuable asset a practitioner has to sell. The most important of these are former patients and other professionals in the community. The more varied the referral sources, the more valuable the practice is.

The characteristics of the purchaser are of particular importance. There should be some similarity between the seller and the purchaser along the dimensions of personality, credentials, special interests, and/or training/experience. Differences are to be expected, perhaps even welcomed, but some connecting handle of similarity must be established.

With that as a guide, a procedure for effecting a transition may be considered. The circumstances of transition planning will have a significant impact on the valuation of a sale. For example, if the seller expects simply to turn over the keys to his office with its furnishings, equipment, and telephone number and no more, the practice is likely to have less value. If, on the other hand, the seller agrees to contact former patients and referral sources to introduce his successor, and further agrees to be present for one to two years or longer in order to work with the buyer and help solidify his acceptance within the community, the more valuable the practice is likely to be. A rule of thumb for beginning negotiation of price of a practice is the gross revenue of one year's practice, or an average of three to five years' practice revenues. Often the price is related to how it is to be paid. Usually, a two-to-three-year purchase payment agreement is most useful. That is, it is agreed that a 33 to 50 percent down payment will be made and that the remainder is to be paid off over a two-to-three-year period. This arrangement builds in an incentive to the seller to help the buyer, and reassures the buyer of the seller's continuing interest in the buyer's success. It is also likely to have certain tax advantages. The price of the practice might be influenced, too, by the competitive circumstances extant in the particular community. However, setting a price related to certain contingencies to be established by actual experience over a period of two to three years may be the fairest and safest method to be employed.

Generally, the practice of a solo practitioner is not likely to be of much value beyond the physical furniture and equipment remaining unless the practitioner is available over a period of time to effect an operationally real transition.

A more valuable practice is a highly specialized one, where the purchaser is well trained and experienced in the same specialization, particularly when the purchaser's training and experience are demonstrable so that his credibility will be easily established within the referral community.

A variation on the sale of a practice is for a senior practitioner to recruit and select a junior partner and work with him with the intent of turning the practice over to him within a specified time span.

Management consultants and attorneys experienced in drawing up contracts for this kind of sale are invaluable sources of advice and guidance. Potential sellers and buyers would be well advised to shop for an appropriate professional adviser.

This chapter has reviewed the practical tasks of running a practice in a businesslike and professional way. Central to the discussion was the emphasis on the need for planning and thinking through the purposes of each aspect of the practice.

The next chapter discusses the managment and control of a private practice.

CHAPTER 7

Controlling a Private Practice

A self-directed practice includes control over the circumstances of the practice.

AFTER HE HAS been in practice awhile, the practice has a tendency to rule the therapist. It is preferable for the therapist to control his practice. For one thing, his own security and sense of well-being will be enhanced in that stance. After all, autonomy and mastery are the hallmarks of good mental health, are especially components of all professionalism, and are central attractions of private practice.

Among the issues around which practice control focuses are (1) size of practice including number of patients in caseload, number of appointments to schedule per day, week, and year, and how to manage time; (2) length of sessions, and to "take a break or not to break" between sessions; (3) frequency of sessions with any one patient or family or group; (4) setting, announcing, and collecting fees and policy regarding failed or broken appointments; (5) scheduling vacations, conferences, workshops, and other continuing education; and (6) consultation for the therapist, serving as a consultant to other professionals, group consultation and/or seminars, and monitoring the effectiveness of one's practice.

Normally, when therapists are beginning their practices, their anxieties center on whether they will ever have enough work to sustain them. By the time a practice matures, however, the concern tends to become "How can I get time for myself?" No matter how long a practice has been in existence and no matter how successful, it rarely proceeds at an even pace. Referrals may come in bunches separated by long "dry spells." Patients improve and terminate, sometimes in bunches that leave gaps in the appointment schedule. The dry spells and the periods when there are gaps in the schedule make the therapists nervous; some even question their competence or, if they are paranoid enough, wonder what they're doing wrong and if nasty rumors are floating about them in the community. A real event, like the awful tragedy of a suicide, homicide, or a spectacular fire-setting involving one's patient, can shake a therapist's confidence—above and beyond the human pain he experiences from the incident. He may take a dry spell or a number of terminations as a sign of community recognition of ineptitude.

And, of course, there are times when the vicissitudes of a therapist's own personal life may render him less than fully efficient. It's pretty tough to deal with a patient's depression while wrestling with one's own mourning process. All of us know that even so common a pain as a toothache can distract us from giving our patients full attention. Patients may sense a loss of empathy and emotional investment and leave. These real deficits, though temporary, can impact on one's practice seriously. Indeed, any therapist who suffers from heavy chronic depression probably should not attempt private practice. The psychological and economic risks are too great. And a time of temporary depression or anxiety state is not the right time to begin a practice. Better to wait for a more propitious moment. It does help to have an upbeat personality, or at least to have that appearance, in building a practice. Somehow, organizations and institutions seem better able to tolerate and/or support people who would otherwise appear too down to function well.

But most who enter private practice have their personalities reasonably under control, and suffer through the ups and downs that are the natural flow pattern of a practice using whatever coping mechanisms they can. There are some common coping mechanisms in private practice that are better than others. Some less desirable mechanisms that may be used when just beginning a practice or during dry spells are to expand the interview session time beyond what has been planned for and agreed to, to give "free" sessions, to "forget" to collect fees or to offer extraordinarily low fees, and to "forgive" failed appointments or frequent cancellations too easily. At the other end of the spectrum when there are too many referrals other undesirable coping mechanisms may include: lengthening the workday, increasing the number of work days, conducting as many as 60 or more interviews a week, as though in a frenzy to make up for dry spells in the past or anticipated in the future. "Never turn a referral away" becomes a kind of religious imperative, for fear the referral source will dry up—or "never have a waiting list" or "Never refer to another therapist." Most experienced therapists have been guilty of using both kinds of coping mechanisms—stretching sessions out, "forgetting" or cutting fees, giving "free" sessions, and fretting that their practice is on the rocks, then letting their schedule build up to as many as 60 or 70 sessions per week. One colleague commented that the latter bordered on a suicidal gesture, and many would agree. (Indeed, one of the more tragic examples that comes to mind is a colleague who suffered a devastating stroke. He had been seeing patients from 7 a.m. through 10 p.m. six days a week. For awhile many admired his "success" and his energy. No more!)

It is far better to set guidelines for one's self from the start and to do one's best to work within them. The specific guidelines will be most influenced by the kind of practice or treatment modalities one feels best equipped to use. Treatment modalities and styles are likely to change over a lifetime of practice as a result of constant learning, of changes in thinking that may especially be generated by research developments, and as a result of one's own personal changes in preference and skills. For example, a therapist may begin practice with a special interest in treating children and their families or in group therapy. Later, interests may shift toward couple and family therapy. Twenty years later the same therapist may be most interested in working with problems associated with middle age and aging in a one-to-one modality. With the recent reawakening of interest in hypnosis, more therapists use it as an adjunctive method to reduce physical and emotional pain and even to shorten the length of time required for therapy. Probably the most prevalent form of therapy practiced is psychoanalytically informed. The therapeutic relationship usually is dynamically intense, and the length of treatment contact a year or more in duration. It would not be unusual in a practice for half the patients who are referred to terminate treatment within six months, while one-third continue for more than two years.

To illustrate, one therapist describes this practice as follows. His caseload consists of about 30 individuals, most of whom are seen for one visit per week, with 20 percent having two or more visits weekly. This means that he holds 40 to 45 sessions per week. His sessions are scheduled to last 45 minutes each, though he allows himself some flexibility to extend a session in times of crisis or in work with couples and families. On this basis he can schedule nine appointments per day, five days a week or 10 visits per day for four days a week and five visits on one shorter day. He averages approximately 175 to 195 visits per month or 2000 visits a year.

With the type of treatment he offers and the nature of his caseload, a comfortable schedule is 35 to 45 visits a week. For therapists who work extensively with children or severely acting-out or decompensated adults, 30 to 35 visits a week might be a more suitable workload. For those who work primarily with groups, probably two sessions a day of 1½ hours each would be maximum, in addition to three or four individual sessions daily. Obviously, individual therapists differ markedly in their physical and mental energy levels and in their biorhythmic cycles. Wise therapists know their energy level and cycle and pace themselves accordingly.

Wallace's survey of more than 350 social workers in private practice as reported in 1977 revealed that more than 200 were in full-time practice (defined as holding 20 or more sessions per week). About three-quarters had a psychoanalytic theoretical base, about half relied on psychosocial theory, and about one-third employed family theories. Sixty-five percent of their time was spent in individual interviews, 18 percent in husband-wife interviews, 7 percent in group treatment, 6 percent in family treatment, and 2 percent in joint interviews other than husband-wife. The typical full-time practitioner held 32 sessions per week.[31]

The first step in controlling a practice is to structure time so that it can be controlled—in one's own and one's patients' interest. The workweek will need to be blocked out day by day, including, usually, some evening time, some weekend time, and time off. Even though in beginning a practice one may have very little time filled, it's better to plan out the time and consolidate appointments into blocks, each of which may eventually be filled in. The blocking of a workweek may look like Figure 7.1.

This figure represents a possible 48-hour week if every session is filled. It allows two evenings and a Saturday morning with Tuesday and Friday mornings off. Generally, the heaviest demand for time is in the later afternoon and evening and Saturday or, sometimes, close to the lunch hour or before 8 a.m.

Variations on this basic blocking are related to offering

Figure 7.1   Blocking of a Workweek

Time	Mon.	Tues.	Wed.	Thurs.	Fri.	Sat.
8 a.m.						
9 a.m.						
10 a.m.						
11 a.m.						
12 a.m.						
Lunch						
1 p.m.						
2 p.m.						
3 p.m.						
4 p.m.						
5 p.m.						
6 p.m.						
Dinner						
7 p.m.						
8 p.m.						
9 p.m.						

a 50-minute session or a 45-minute session. Some variations follow:

1. The scholarly comfortable schedule: 50-minute sessions, nine sessions per day, 40-minute lunch, 10-minute break between appointments, 8 a.m. to 5:20 p.m. per day.

A.M.	P.M.
8–8:50	12:30–1:20
9–9:50	1:30–2:20
10–10:50	2:30–3:20
11–11:50	3:30–4:20
	4:30–5:20

2. The therapist killer: 50-minute sessions, 11 sessions per day, 35-minute lunch, no breaks (except by cancellation or planned "unfilled" time), 8 a.m. to 5:45 p.m. per day.

A.M.	P.M.
8–8:50	12:45–1:35
8:50–9:40	1:35–2:25
9:40–10:30	2:25–3:15
10:30–11:20	3:15–4:05
11:20–12:10	4:05–4:55
	4:55–5:45

3. The therapist's "slow death" schedule: 45-minute sessions, 11 sessions per day, 35-minute lunch, 5-minute break between sessions, 8 a.m. to 5:40 p.m.

A.M.	P.M.
8–8:45	12:45–1:30
8:50–9:35	1:35–2:20
9:40–10:25	2:25–3:10
10:30–11:15	3:15–4
11:20–12:10	4:05–4:50
Lunch	4:55–5:40

4. The therapist's "early death" schedule: 45 minutes per session, 12 sessions per day, 30-minute lunch, no breaks, 8 a.m. to 5:30 p.m. except for "open" sessions "by plan."

5. The therapist's "life-preserving" schedule: 45 minutes per session, 10 sessions per day, 45-minute lunch (easily extended to 1½ hours), 15-minute break between sessions for bathroom, telephone, exercise, note writing, thinking, resting, even napping or quick errands, dictation of letters, signing letters, etc.

A.M.	P.M.
8–8:45	1:30–2:15
9–9:45	2:30–3:15
10–10:45	3:30–4:15
11–11:45	4:30–5:15
12–12:45	5:30–6:15

Perhaps it is not so obvious, but any therapist who attempts to fit himself into any one of these straight-jacketing time schedules rigidly should probably not be practicing at all, but should be in treatment or in another line of work. Unfortunately, many therapists evaluate their personal *success* in terms of how many treatment hours they can fill. It is an easy enough trap into which to fall. Size of practice and interview count are a very seductive but ultimately foolish and misleading measure of a therapist's success or competence. And focus upon such a measure is ultimately self-destructive. If a practice is very heavy, it is likely to sap every bit of the therapist's energy. If it is "too light," it is likely to raise the therapist's anxiety level. In general, anxiety over too light a schedule is likely to be less self-destructive than attempting to carry too heavy a schedule.

It is true that the private practice of psychotherapy is a "piece work" business, and income is directly related to patients seen. Therefore, a therapist must determine what he considers an acceptable or "good enough" income and relate this to size of fee and number of sessions worked. But as a guideline for a reasonable number of therapeutic hours to work in a week, without unduly draining the therapist of energy, 40 sessions per week seems a reasonable norm. If one cannot charge a high enough fee working this number of hours to satisfy income requirements, perhaps other employment ought to be sought.

It is wise to think in terms of controlling one's time, since this is basically what the private practitioner sells. Clearly, his expertise must in some way enrich each segment of time in such a way that the patients think it's worth buying. There are therapists who don't see their therapeutic intervention activities in quite such nominal measures. For example, some therapists will cut a session short or extend a session for hours, depending on the material being tackled. But most are bound by some conventional measuring system-most commonly, time = money charged or valued. It is essential to recognize that this is a convention which we—patient and therapist—agree to abide by, rather than some magical curative phenomenon in its own right which it is not.

Setting up a schedule, for a week and for a day, is one convenient way for a therapist to control his time in an orderly way. And to charge for it. A preference for a 45-minute session may be based on the observation that usually most of what is "productive" tends to be covered in such a time span, and that it is a unit of time that can be relatively easily manipulated into suitable larger blocks. For example, two 45-minute sessions can be used for a group therapy session, a business lunch, a seminar, an emergency shopping expedition, etc. Or, if one's practice involves hospital visits, the 45-minute session is likely to fit better into a daily schedule. Or, where one has more than one office, the 45-minute session permits greater scheduling flexibility for travel assuming appropriate proximity of offices. And, finally, when patients' schedules require clustering of appointments around the lunch hour or in the late afternoon or early evening, the 45-minute module permits greater flexibility.

In general, each therapist will need to think carefully about how to block out time throughout a week, leaving some time for evening appointments, some close to the lunch hour, and some during the weekend. But adequate time off must especially be planned for, too. The 45-minute session seems the most useful time module, permitting the placement of two to-

gether, or the scheduling of breaks between sessions, or planning to leave time unfilled in blocks that are adequate to be usa-
ble for other purposes including rest periods, note writing,
dictation, phone contacts, etc.

In addition to day-to-day scheduling, the wise therapist
will schedule vacation, conference, workshop, and other times
off well in advance. A dentist recently reported that he regularly blocks out one or two weeks on his calendar after every
60 days he is scheduled to work, to be set aside for vacation, or
R & R—in addition to any legal holidays and also any professional workshops, conferences, seminars, etc., which he re-
gards as work. The blocked-off time is his to do with as he
wishes. Psychotherapists might well pay close attention to this
approach to managing and controlling time. Of course, dentists
are even more obsessive-compulsive than psychotherapists.
But sometimes it is useful to put our psychic devices to work in
the service of our own real needs.

Frequency of sessions with any one patient is a technical
issue about which theoreticians differ. Psychoanalytic theorists believe that frequent sessions, like four or five sessions
per week, tend to intensify the transference and permit exploration of the depths of unconscious mental life more fully.
Other theorists whose therapeutic goals are directed more
toward behavioral change or problem solving than toward
strictly intrapsychic personality exploration are likely to
schedule sessions with less frequency, or will experiment with
varying frequencies.

Time, of course, like almost any other phenomenon, may
be put to therapeutic usefulness. Many years ago Bruno Bet-
telheim, a great child analyst, lectured his students regarding
the virtue or lack of virtue of the 50-minute hour. He pointed
out that there are times when great therapeutic advantage
might be gained by working with a patient for hours on end continuously, while at other times a session might just as well be
concluded after a few moments. His point was that the 50-min-

ute hour was a convention dictated more by pragmatic economic and practice management needs than by therapeutic necessity. Therapists who use the marathon model of treatment
believe that often this is an opportunity to get at psychological
material more quickly and effectively than in many other ways.
Certainly, most therapists encounter crisis situations where
they will stay with a patient for prolonged periods during
which critical issues may be worked on and through. Most experienced therapists with active practices will recall times
when they saw a patient seven days a week and were in telephone contact, in addition, to help the patient through some ter-
rible time in his life.

Obviously, frequency of sessions is determined on the basis of both therapeutic judgment and economic considerations.
For the therapist who sees patients more frequently and over a
protracted time span, there is need for fewer referrals to maintain his practice. Therapists who tend to see patients less frequently and for brief periods require more referrals, and they
need referrals more regularly.

Aside from classical psychoanalytic therapists, most therapists see patients once or twice weekly and cases will continue for six months to a year or longer. The implication for
management and building of practice are immediately apparent. The classical analyst who sees analytic cases almost exclusively for four to five sessions per week and three to six
years or longer will require fewer than 10 cases to be fully
scheduled. (Not long ago, a very famous and well-respected analyst who recently died in her late eighties reported that she
had analyzed a total of only 30 people during the course of her
lengthy and successful career.) The therapist who uses the one-
to-one model and sees his patients once a week for six months
to a year will require 40 to 50 referrals a year to be fully scheduled and will experience a turnover of clientele on the average
of every nine months. He will need approximately three to six
referrals per month after building up to a full caseload to main-

tain it, which would allow for ordinary turnover of caseload and for attrition of referrals who choose not to engage themselves in ongoing work. Generally, more than two out of three referrals will follow through. After one has been in practice awhile, new referrals are augmented by the return of former patients for either brief or extended series of visits. Unfortunately, a flow of referrals is rarely even or predictable, and therapists often do have to juggle their schedules to accommodate bunched-up referrals or former patients. However, if one follows the guide of holding approximately 40 sessions per week, when this number varies up to 50 or more sessions per week, the therapist ought seriously to be thinking about referring to other therapists or bringing associates into his practice. Generally, unless there is some special overriding reason, it is undesirable to create a waiting list because of the inconvenience and sometimes serious risk to patients. For some therapists, of course, a waiting list is a status symbol.

Therapists who choose to practice primarily or exclusively group therapy obviously require a greater flow of referrals and may create a waiting list in order to form a viable group over a period of a month or two. Perhaps this referrals factor accounts for the fact that the majority of private practitioners engage primarily in one-to-one therapy, rarely working with groups, in spite of the fact that group therapy is far more lucrative on an hourly basis. Or there may be an economic disincentive to forming therapy groups if the frequency of referrals is limited. That is, if one can fill 18 therapy hours individually and charge, let us say, $50 per session, gross income will be $900 per week, while if one sees the same 18 patients in three groups each consisting of six patients and charges each person $25 per session, gross income is cut in half. Of course, it would require less than one-third the actual hours, and therefore hourly gross income would almost triple. This observation suggests that the economic disincentive decreases as the rate of referrals increases. Many group therapists and others would argue that the economics of group therapy are not as important as the virtues inherent in the method itself.

For many patients group therapy may be more viable than individual treatment, and for others group therapy may be a valuable adjunct to individual treatment. To make group therapy economically feasible in private practice, a steady and large flow of referrals is essential. To make hard-number estimates of how many referrals are necessary is difficult. However, observation suggests that group therapists are likely to generate requisite numbers of referrals more readily by joining with other therapists rather than attempting to go solo.

Thus far, focus has been on the development of a full-time private practice. However, much of what this chapter is about is applicable to anyone planning and managing a part-time practice as well. In an article entitled "Part-Time Private Practice for the Reluctant Entrepreneur," psychologist Steven G. Weinrach wrote, "My time is far more structured than it was when I was just teaching. I could schedule my reading and research activities whenever I wished. That is not the case any longer. Having made a commitment to a part-time practice means that I must be available to my clients both for office hours as well as phone calls." He goes on, however, to illustrate what was earlier cited as a poor coping mechanism associated with beginning a practice, namely, "I find that with my school aged clients I am spending considerable time in conferences with their counselors and parents for which I choose not to charge, by and large. But, thus far, I have enjoyed the experience."[32] This comment probably reveals his ambivalence and self-doubt about being an entrepreneur and his efforts to cope with them. Why be "reluctant" about private practice? And why not charge for time, particularly when time needs to be "far more structured" than before?

Nevertheless, the need to manage time and control one's practice even though it is part-time is well illustrated in Weinrach's article. And the variations in practice management requirements in relation to different methodologies employed and types of clientele seen are also revealed.

Fee Setting and Collection

The process by which the amount of fees charged for specified services filters through the professional community often seems sinister and a marvel. Most professions, including medicine, dentistry, and the law, shy away from publishing fee schedules for specific services. Legal suits have been brought against some professional groups for efforts at what appears to be price fixing, and most professional associations have committees to deal with complaints of price gouging by individual practitioners. An accountant has suggested that if only a small proportion of one's patients complain about the size of their fee or refuse services because of fees, then one is probably not charging enough. Not infrequently colleagues have been guilty of measuring their popularity, worth, success, or reputation by the size of their fees. This is a ridiculous measure for self-assessment. Many therapists have strongly ambivalent feelings about charging higher fees or increasing fees as their experience increases and as an inflationary economy continuously erodes the "real" value of money.

All in all, the setting of professional fees appears to be arbitrary rather than rational. It really doesn't make sense that a very recent entrant into a professional practice of any kind should charge fees equivalent to those of a highly experienced and seasoned practitioner. Yet that is the general practice among professions, except perhaps in law firms. There is a relatively wide variance in "billing per hour" between younger and older partners in major law firms. Advice to younger psychotherapists entering into private practice is to charge whatever they think the prevailing fee rate is in their community. Nevertheless, widely given advice also recommends that they modify fees downward initially, but by plan, in cases of hardship for patients and in order to fill their time. If a therapist employs a sliding scale in setting his fees, does that constitute a "means test"—"Can you afford such and such?"—and if so, isn't that inherently demeaning? There may be an implication that if the patient were really successful, he could "afford" whatever the therapist charged. Now, just as such a measure as size of fee is an inherently ridiculous measure by which to assess a psychotherapist's value, so is the ability of a patient to pay a given fee a ridiculous measure of a patient's value—or, God knows, need! Yet in our competitive society, judgments are often made in these emotionally irrational ways.

In the private practice of psychotherapy it is vital to identify things as they are and not to hedge or dissemble. This is especially so in the matter of fee setting. Fee setting has to do with the management by the therapist of his income, and perhaps his greed, in the context of the market for his services. English translation: therapists generally set their fees at a level that their patients are willing to pay when there is a competitive situation where choices are available to the patient. In instances where choices are limited or nonexistent for the patient, where his resources are sharply limited, or where the patient's judgment is impaired, therapists must rely on an inner sense of fairness, morality, and a humane life philosophy. It is a source of puzzlement how a professional peer review committee can evaluate "price gouging" without having a "price schedule" that meets general standards of acceptability. The insurance industry collects data on fees for services in a given community and establishes "usual and ordinary" fees for specific services at which insurance companies reimburse for services to patients covered under their policies. These figures are usually only a vague representation of reality, and are generally less than what is in fact charged.

The Chinese have quite another approach to fee setting for health services that some health insurance companies in the United States have adopted, especially in Health Maintenance

Organizations (HMO). Conventionally fees are based on "input," usually measured by credentials, experience, and previous successes. The Chinese seek to reward, or pay, health care professionals in relation to "output," meaning results in a given instance.

The more ordinary approach to fee setting, less exciting and interesting than this latter, is related to prevailing charges for similar services provided by people with roughly equivalent preparation (with credentials requiring equivalent investments of time, money, and energy) for which the community at large generally is willing to pay—no matter what the outcome. An example of this model is the surgeon who excises a cancer and charges a "standard" fee for the surgery although the patient may die. Others are the psychotherapist who invests hours and energy in working with a family that ultimately dissolves in divorce and a therapist who struggles valiantly to lift an overwhelming depression but the patient succeeds in suicide—with both therapists "billing for an hourly rate" despite the sad outcome. Most of us opt for the ordinary method of payment in psychotherapy—that is, we bill for the time we invest. We agree to sell our services in this package of "time equals money."

A professional who is interested in determining what the size of his fee ought to be in a given community might follow a simple procedure. Call a few therapists of varying professions as though one were a prospective patient and ask what the person's fee is. It is a minor bit of dissembling, of course, but it is the simplest way to determine "going rates" in an area. One must still set his own fee above, below, or at the average discovered by this simple survey. If one is the only mental health professional in private practice in an area, he may inquire regarding fees charged by public or private clinics or agencies. If these, too, are absent, he may inquire about what doctors, dentists, lawyers, or others charge for specific procedures, estimate the time involved, and extrapolate accordingly.

Or a quite different approach is simply to compute the income one thinks is appropriate to his skill, experience, and age, divide by a reasonable number of hours one expects to work, allowing for vacations and conferences, and use the resulting figure as one's regular hourly fee or fee per session.

Usually, psychiatrists' fees per session are higher than psychologists' fees per session, which in turn are higher than clinical social workers' fees per session. However, this rule need not be binding. The actual market response from consumers is the important and telling consideration. Private practice is, after all, a small business at least partially responsive to the laws of supply and demand in the market place. In 1982, in the Midwest, psychiatric fees for 45 minutes ranged within $60 to $80; clinical psychologists' ranged within $50 to $75, and clinical social workers' ranged within $40 to $65. These rates probably are at variance with those charged in the East and the Southwest and on the West Coast, and there is considerable variation within regions, particularly between rural and urban population centers. Fees tend to be higher in areas where there are fewer professional resources; apparently following the Adam Smith rules of supply and demand.

In testimony presented in December 1982 before the House Ways and Means Subcommittee on Health (H. R. 5092), data were submitted showing the cost of therapy provided by psychologists and psychiatrists according to CHAMPUS data.

Table 7.1: COST OF THERAPY

Description	Type of Practitioner	Average Paid
Psychotherapy, verbal 50 min. (outpatient)	Psychiatrist	$50.82
	Psychologist	47.51
Psychotherapy, adult or child 45–50 min. (outpatient)	Psychiatrist	57.58
	Psychologist	55.75
Psychotherapy, verbal 25 min. (inpatient)	Psychiatrist	31.77
	Psychologist	26.09
Psychotherapy, adult or child, 45–50 min., Hospital or other facility (inpatient)	Psychiatrist	62.24
	Psychologist	56.91

Source: *Behavior Today Newsletter*, 1983, vol. 13, no. 52 (Jan. 3), p. 7.

A fee survey (Table 7.2) was also conducted by *Behavior Today*.

It is essential for an individual practitioner to set his fee schedule clearly and to be prepared to announce it to patients either when they call to arrange an appointment or not later than the end of the first visit. Indeed, by the end of the first visit all the practical aspects of the patient-therapist "contract" should be spelled out at least verbally. More and more therapists are supplementing this with a written statement given to each patient. The "contract" written or oral, should include fee per visit; length of visit; policy on canceled appointments; policy on failed appointments; policy on vacations, holidays, etc.; policy on insurance reimbursement; policy on fees for telephone calls; policy on how and when payments are to be made.

More and more therapists are asking patients to pay for each session each time to eliminate billing expenses and/or accumulation of large balances. These payments preferably will be made by check, but if made by cash, they will be duly recorded and a receipt will be issued to the patient.

Insurance Reimbursement

Where there is some form of insurance coverage, most therapists prefer to be paid directly by the patient and prepare the appropriate insurance claim forms so that the patient may be reimbursed. In the case of clinical social workers and clinical psychologists especially, but also for clinical psychiatrists and others, the patient should be warned that insurance reimbursement is not always certain, and that the size of reimbursement may be surprisingly low. In general, it is the responsibility of the therapist to do everything in his power to help the patient recover as much as possible in insurance reimbursement, since this is a *right* for which he has paid premiums directly or premi-

Table 7.2:   FEE SURVEY

Social Workers:

INDIVIDUAL THERAPY FEES	FAMILY THERAPY FEES
38%–$50	19%–$35
19%–$35	14.3%–$50
14.3%–$40	14.3%–$40
9.5%–$60	9.5%–$60
9.5%–$45	4.8%–$70
4.8%–$70	4.8%–$65
4.8%–$30	4.8%–$45

COUPLE THERAPY	GROUP THERAPY
23.8%–$40	27.27%–$25
14.3%–$50	18.18%–$20
14.3%–$35	18.18%–$15
9.5%–$65	9.09%–$40
4.8%–$75	9.09%–$30
4.8%–$60	9.09%–$8
4.8%–$55	9.09%–$13 5/month
4.8%–$30	

Marriage and Family/Sex Therapists

GROUP THERAPY	INDIVIDUAL OR COUPLE FEES	FAMILY THERAPY
28.57%–$20	28.57%–$50	28.57%–$50
14.28%–$35	14.28%–$70	14.28%–$45
57% do not offer	14.28%–$55	14.28%–$70
group therapy	14.28%–$45	14.28%–$60
	14.28%–$40	14.28%–$40
	14.28%–$25	14.28%–$25

Counselors/Consultants

INDIVIDUAL THERAPY	COUPLE THERAPY	GROUP THERAPY
25%–$50	37.5%–$50	25%–$30
12.5%–$65	12.5%–$90	12.5%–$50
12.5%–$55	12.5%–$65	12.5%–$20
12.5%–$48	12.5%–$40	12.5%–$40
12.5%–$40	12.5%–$30	12.5%–$8
12.5%–$35		12.5%–$90/mo.
12.5%–$30		
12.5%–$25		

Source: *Behavior Today Newsletter*, 1982, vol 13, no. 42 (Oct. 25), p. 8.

ums have been paid for him as a form of compensation by his employer. Insurance reimbursement for fees for psychotherapy is not a "charity," "a gift," or some sort of "rip-off." It is a system designed to reduce the burden of the high cost of psychotherapy. Insurance is a money pool through which the cost of protecting against the risk of an unanticipated expense is spread, a risk to which all are exposed all the time, but fortunately, one which causes only a few of us to suffer at any one time. It is essential that this concept of health insurance, and especially mental health insurance reimbursements, as a *right* paid for or *earned by the consuming patient* be understood by patient and therapist alike.

The amount of money reimbursed by insurance for psychotherapy fees, however, is rarely as much as 50 percent of the actual fee—and often less. An occasional plan—or combination of two or more plans—may sometimes go as high as 80 percent of cost. Many plans plug in only after a patient has been hospitalized. And for nonmedical therapists many plans require that a patient be seen by a physician who refers, and/or that treatment be supervised by a physician, in order for the patient to receive any reimbursement at all.

Most therapists expect patients to pay the full fee for appointments that are "failed" (no advance notice) or canceled with less than 48 or 72 hours notice. This policy is not treated as punishment of the patient, but as a simple business practice. The therapist reserves time that might have been "sold" to another patient—something like a theater ticket purchased in advance. As a matter of ethical practice, in an instance where a therapist "fills" an appointment that has been canceled in advance, he ought not to charge the canceling patient for the time and should so inform him. Given the delicate psychodynamics of the psychotherapy encounter, it is inappropriate to "double-bill" for the same time—even if neither the canceling patient nor the "filling" patient knows about the other. There is probably no way to enforce such a rule externally, but for their internal integrity, therapists ought to follow the rule as though it were mandated. Some few therapists expect their patients to plan their vacations to coincide with the therapist's. If the patient's vacation does not coincide, he is expected to pay for sessions "missed." Whatever the merits of this practice, it must be explicated at the very beginning of the therapy.

In those instances where fees are not collected at each visit, bills are usually sent on the first day of the month for the preceding month's work. The wise therapist doesn't ignore lagging payments and confronts the patient directly to secure payment in a timely manner. If there is some reason for a delay in payment, the patient and the therapist must discuss this and arrive at a mutually satisfactory agreement in advance as to appropriate arrangements. In the instance of treatment of children or dependent adults where a person other than the patient is responsible for payment, it is not only advisable but essential that an agreement be worked out in advance of initiation of treatment regarding the payment of fees. In the case of a divorced spouse responsible for payment of a spouse's treatment or for treatment of a dependent child, especially one not living with the spouse who is to pay the fee, it is best to have an agreement in writing that is signed and countersigned by all concerned—in advance. If a court order is involved, it is better to have that order completed and in hand before commencing treatment.

In both the short and the long run, this approach is likely best to protect the interests of the dependent patients, the person who is responsible for paying the fee, and the therapist. There are few things worse for a responsible therapist than to be in the position of having invested in a patient and achieved the patient's trust, only to discover too late that external supports for the patient have been withdrawn or were never there. Even when the therapist wants to proceed with a sharply reduced or waived fee, usually the patient will not be able to continue for one or more dynamic reasons. In private practice it is

virtually impossible to "give service" away. The patient re-
gards the "gift" as too great a psychological burden to accept
emotionally.

Fees paid by patients are generally deductible as a medical expense for income tax purposes whether treatment is offered by psychologists, social workers, or psychiatrists. Where
the IRS questions the deduction, it is usually wise for the taxpayer to carry the matter to an IRS supervisor or beyond.

Vacations

Private practioners are their own boss, and they ought to
be a good boss. In a benign, benevolent way they must schedule
themselves for vacations, professional meetings, seminars, consultations, and so on. No one else will do it for them. There is
likely to be considerable resistance to doing it. The awareness
of the "meter ticking away" while one is "unproductive" is
powerful. Yes, phone and rent will still have to be paid while
away, but that should be computed into an annual estimated
budget of income and expense. And for the convenience and
emotional security of patients, one needs to plan in advance
and inform them well in advance what the plans are for vacation, professional meeting absence, etc. While it is not always
technically wise to share with patients why one is away, it is always wise and essential to inform them in advance of planned
absences, how long absences will extend, and when they will
next be seen. As a general rule, patients should have at least a
month's notice of a prolonged absence (a week or more), even if
only a single hour's appointment is directly affected. Most patients need to know internally themselves that their therapist is
around even when they are not seeing him, and they expect and
are reassured to be informed of his whereabouts. Patients also
become concerned when they become aware that their therapist fails to take a vacation.

Most therapists arrange to be in touch with their offices or are available for emergency communication when they are gone from their offices for a week or more. Rarely is their presence required when such arrangements are made. It's when no such arrangements have been made that some patients panic and try to force emergency contact.

Most therapists arrange to have colleagues "cover" for them when they are absent for a week or more. When a patient sees the colleague, the usual custom is for the colleague to charge the patient's customary fee and for the patient to pay the colleague directly. Because of the psychodynamics involved (possibly fostering unnecessary dependency), ordinarily the regular therapist doesn't spell this out in advance, but the colleague who fills in does so on an ad hoc basis as the issue evolves. However, the colleagues had best work out an agreement in advance, so that they at least understand what's what and avoid antagonism that may result from confusion.

Fighting Isolation in Private Practice

In private practice, especially full time, the greatest enemy is isolation and potential professional alienation. No private practitioner can escape this or avoid taking responsibility to combat it. Usually, when beginning a practice, psychotherapists tend to purchase consultation from other professionals—partly in order to learn, partly to have someone hold their hand and allay paralyzing anxiety, and partly in the hopes of eliciting a referral or two from the consultant. As time goes on, anxiety tends to subside and with it the need to have one's hand held. New learning is perceived to be achieved in better ways than through consultation. And the referrals from consultants so rarely materialize that the whole enterprise usually dies of its own weight—canceled meetings, dull, boring meetings for which "there was not time to prepare," and so on.

A far more stimulating approach to learning is to teach others—either by consulting (with the same pitfalls as above) or in organized courses. Another option is to be part of an ongoing seminar with either a paid leader or rotating discussion leadership. Usually, the more stringently demanding of attendance and preparation these are, the more useful and productive.

Group consultation looks good on paper, but rarely works out in practice—unless there is such stringent demandingness.

With all of these, the question still remains—how to monitor one's practice overall. It is money well spent by a therapist to employ a consultant at least once a year to spend a concentrated period of time reviewing written or oral presentations of either the therapist's entire caseload or a substantial sample of it. The review should be a mutual one with a list of benchmarks to be evaluated, including the simple numerical ones—how many cases seen in a year; what's the rate of turnover; what kinds of cases; what cases were the most satisfactory, what the least; where was progress made, where not; why not, why yes; where did one feel shakiest or strongest; in what specific is there uneasiness; what elements for comparison might be identified to assess one's progress over the following year. It may be that one or two cases may be selected, or one or two categories of case, to be followed closely with an eye to discussng them with the monitor-consultant or with another colleague. This kind of regular self-evaluation, especially if it is integrated with reading and discussion of old or contemporary theorists, is a basic aid in averting the doldrums, burn-out, or some of the more pernicious coping or defensive mechanisms that often afflict unwary isolated therapists.

Serious burn-out blahs can lead to depression, withdrawal, and even suicide. In middle age, therapists may mask these feelings with the garden-variety symptomatic behavior of proving one's masculinity or femininity—inside or outside the consulting room. The depression may still be lurking just around the corner, and may even be aggravated by embarrassing acting-out behavior.

Another burn-out syndrome is the "know-it-all" or "maven" or "I've finally distilled the most complete and apt theory to explain behavior and treatment process ever" syndrome. This syndrome may be as serious as an obvious depression—though less life-threatening to the bearer, more life-threatening to those around him. They may verge on death by boredom or death by suppressed rage—particularly if the bearer of the syndrome is in a position of power, which is often the case since it is associated with middle age.

The best antidotes to these two symptoms of burn-out are exposure to confrontation by sympathetic and friendly colleagues. They may be prevented through a regular process of self-evaluation undertaken with the help of a friendly outsider beginning early in practice and in a strictly self-disciplined way continued preferably annually throughout one's career no matter which way the career goes. One important way to maintain one's professional vitality as one moves along is to find younger therapists for whom one may fill the role of mentor. Here the caveat is to stand ready always for the mentee to break loose into greater independence, leaving one to find new youngsters to help along.

And, of course, more personal psychotherapy is always a possibility. "Stress Management" or "Anti-Burn-out" workshops may help, but many would question their effectiveness.

The control of one's practice is a never-ending task which should begin at the very beginning of private work. One must "own" one's practice rather than be "owned" by it. This is the sine qua non for making a successful, satisfying, lucrative lifelong career. The key is to recognize that one is responsible for one's self in a fully adult way.

In the next chapter, discussion continues about what it's like to be in private practice.

CHAPTER 8

The Course of a Private Practice—From Beginning to Maturity

Warning: A taste of private practice may be habit-forming

WHAT IS IT REALLY LIKE to be in private practice? What kinds of people are likely to be seen? How do therapists feel? What is it like when beginning in practice? What's it like when one is well into a practice?

Beginnings are usually exciting but worrisome. Experience suggests that the earliest patients referred to a new practitioner tend to present the most difficult and complex problems to be encountered anywhere. This finding has been confirmed by colleagues in private practice and by those who have opened a new clinic or other agency service. Perhaps the opening of any new facility implies that a need exists and that there is a backlog of patients in serious need. Or it may be that a new practitioner is approached by patients who have already burned out other therapists. Whatever the explanation, the therapist in his newly opened practice needs to be prepared for the worst: suicidal, homicidal individuals; disruptive, incorrigible children; severely sadomasochistic marriages; potential anorexias; severely paranoid or intensely acting-out adolescents;

167

and pathological states that one may vaguely recall having read about but have never seen before. Initially, most practitioners are not able to limit their cases to a narrow area of specialization. The pressure to develop a practice makes it difficult to turn any referral down. This may seem to make it impossible to fulfill the earlier proposition offered that when one goes into private practice, one ought to be well prepared for the kinds of cases one is to serve there. And indeed, practicalities of life may supersede this principle a bit at first. Nevertheless, a well-trained, reasonably experienced, personally stable therapist is likely to be able to handle the problems presented to him.

Most people start their practice on a part-time basis. They either use an office in their home or sublet space from another professional. The very first appointment with a private patient is generally anticipated with considerable anxiety. Questions of how to set and collect the fee, even when it's already been thought out, cause a certain amount of anxiety. One way to control the anxiety is for the new practitioner to come to his office earlier than the scheduled appointment to familiarize himself with the space and psychologically *lay claim* to the space so that he feels it is his office, at least for the next few moments. As we shall see later, the quality of one's office may be of far more significance to the therapist than to the patient, at least initially, assuming that privacy and reasonable comfort are provided. Naturally, architecture, furniture, etc., will express much about the therapist, his style and even his personality, and these may eventually become grist for the mill of treatment.

It is generally a good idea to observe the usual social amenities when a new patient arrives. It is not unprofessional to shake hands with a patient, to be pleasantly cordial, being sure to say the patient's name loudly and clearly, introducing one's self loudly and clearly, attempting to make the patient comfortable in the office with the seating arrangements. While these suggestions may appear gratuitous to an experienced therapist, we all may bear the reminder, since we may react to the anxiety of a new experience by forgetting even deeply ingrained basics. The line between being cordial and being seductive may sometimes be difficult to draw. Let us have no misunderstanding; there is no suggestion of a seductive approach to the client, but rather a cordial, friendly one. Whatever the patient's problem, he is likely to be especially anxious in his first appointment. The well-known phenomenon of "crazy anxiety" is the fear on the part of the patient that he must be "crazy" if he's coming to see a therapist or that the therapist will discover that the patient is "crazy." In the effort to establish a cordial and comfortable ambiance, the therapist must not shy away from talking about the problem that brings the patient to him. Probably the most appropriate and most successful way to set the patient at ease and to increase one's own comfort is to get into the work as quickly as possible.

It is in the first visit that the patient should get an idea of how the therapist is going to work and begin the process of identifying his problem and approaches toward its resolution. For the therapist's own comfort, it is generally a wise idea to keep rather extensive notes of the initial visits of the first patients one sees in private practice for review at a later date. As the therapist engages the patient in review of his problem and a treatment approach to it, the therapist's own anxieties about seeing the patient privately will likely subside very quickly and his professional training and experience will evidence themselves.

Because most professionals entering private practice have come from an experience where they have had supervision and where much of their work was reviewed by others, there is a tendency initially to feel as though one's work in private practice is somehow being scrutinized by another person. The idea of an "illusory supervisor" may well describe this phenomenon. Some practitioners who have received a referral from another therapist carry with them the idea that they will have to report on their activity to the referring agent. These feelings are strongest when beginning a practice. Eventually, the therapist will free himself, as he becomes accustomed to relying on self-scrutiny and finds ways to monitor himself independently. Perhaps the "illusory supervisor" is really a "transitional object" to be separated from in good time.

Settling practical working matters during the first visit will make everyone more comfortable. These include setting the amount of the fee and arrangements for collecting it, and explaining about the length of a visit, usually 45 to 50 minutes for individual sessions, or an hour to an hour and a half for sessions with couples, families, or groups. By the end of the first visit, or certainly by the end of the third or fourth visit, the frequency of appointments should be established. Usually beginning practitioners tend to be more rigid in their expectations of themselves and of their patients. With more experience and increased security, it is easier to be flexible, as for example in regard to frequency of visits.

Although initially a practitioner may expect referrals of a considerable degree of complexity, he will also find that private patients tend to be strongly motivated for treatment, more so than agency or clinic patients tend to be. The patient's expectations also are likely to be greater. These expectations include that the practitioner be experienced and knowledgeable, that the setting be pleasant but professional, that the service be immediate, or at least responsive to the patient's need, and that there be a continuity of service from the therapist. The patient expects to be considered as a special individual, not just another case. The professional's interest, or lack thereof, in the patient will be sensed immediately, and of course will have an important bearing on the progress of therapy. By way of illustration, a colleague reported that a patient came to him recently after terminating with another therapist. He explained how the previous therapist had consulted some notes on his desk and started to talk with this patient until it became evident to the patient that the therapist was reading notes about another patient. The patient was outraged and terminated treatment almost instantaneously. (And, of course, he needed to test the genuineness of the new therapist's interest.) Practitioners just entering into private practice are not likely to have this problem, but it does dramatically illustrate the importance in the private practice setting of the patient's wish for and demand for highly individualized interest on the part of the therapist.

Naturally, there is no way to tell what kind of a case will be the first referred in a new practice. Initial referrals may vary in the way they are presented in relation to the particular profession that the private practitioner represents. A psychiatrist, for example, may get a referral for a person suffering from what is descriptively an acute depression; a psychologist may be referred a child with some kind of a learning disability; a social worker may be referred a family exploding at the seams. When one gets down to the actualities, however, the similarities are likely to be greater than the differences between the individuals and families who are referred, although the way the problem or the patient is prelabeled and initially defined may be tailored to the respective professions.

The first private referral that came to one therapist was from an older and experienced person. She called and asked him if he'd be interested in seeing an 18-year-old boy whose mother she had been treating in a psychiatric clinic. After she had described his problems, the novice agreed to take the case. He explained that he had not rented an office yet, but had a "study" in the basement of his suburban home that was private and relatively soundproof. The colleague was supportive and reassured him that that would probably be okay. They arranged for the mother to call at home, which she did. The novice realized that he was unexpectedly anxious on the phone in spite of his having had years of experience in taking telephone referrals in agencies and clinics. He found himself struggling not to apologize about seeing her son in an office in his home. A few days later, the boy arrived at the office and they began their work. At first, the therapist caught himself being more preoccupied with what the young patient would think of the "study" office than in observing him. Fortunately, these feelings quickly subsided as they got down to the business at hand—identifying the problems and working out an approach to them. Much later in treatment, the therapist learned from his young patient that in his initial anxiety about beginning treatment he had not even been aware of the office. That had been the therapist's problem, not the patient's, as was so easy to see in hindsight.

The 18-year-old was a poor student, possibly organically retarded. (This was long before the concept of "learning disability" became popular.) As it turned out, his familial situation was one where he had very little support from his father; he had an overambitious, overprotective mother. His intelligence was average. What he needed was reassuring support and help in finding direction for a life plan. He needed clarification of his realistic potentials and limitations. This male therapist served as a role model for him, offered him support, an idea about what it was like to be a man, and what it was like to make one's way through life successfully. The treatment plan did not involve his gaining great insight into his intrapsychic functioning, but rather was focused on practical steps that he might take to break away from his mother, establish an occupational plan, and learn how to regard himself as a viable, acceptable person capable of success in life. This proved to be an appropriate approach. Over a period of two years of once-a-week contacts he attained a degree of success vocationally, found a girlfriend who helped him to break away from his mother, and was able to develop into a socially and vocationally competent self-respecting young adult. Initially, the new private practitioner was filled with self-doubts as to the efficacy of his efforts. He had been trained to think in psychoanalytic terms. Could he regard this treatment, which was not "insight-oriented," as doing the right thing by the patient? After all, this was a private case, so perhaps it deserved something "extra special," like psychoanalysis. The youngster would have needed frequent visits over several years to conform to the psychoanalytic model of that time. It turned out that the procedure chosen—a problem-solving approach offering emotional support, clarification, a model with whom to identify, and cognitive direction in making choices and decisions that would help him to be independent—worked very well, probably better than an insight-oriented treatment. A psychiatrist, a psychologist, or a clinical social worker might have done the very same thing that this young man's therapist did. The psychologist might have been conflicted about not offering more specific vocational testing and counseling. The psychiatrist might have doubted the importance of the case because of its relative simplicity. And the psychoanalytically oriented social worker, especially one who had been steeped in psychoanalytic supervision, might have been plagued by the "illusory supervisor." But a competent psychiatrist or psychologist or social worker probably would have offered similar supportive, directive help to this young man with interventions aimed at increasing his sense of self-esteem, increasing his capacity to separate himself from his mother, and enlarging his perception of himself as an adequate young man, although individual and professional style might have varied.

Almost simultaneously with the referral of this young man, a 30-year-old woman was referred to the same clinican by her physician. Once again, the therapist was anxious during the telephone discussion with the physician, who happened to be his own family doctor, but this time did not have to seek reassurance about his office. However, another source of anxiety was stirred. This would be a young, attractive woman whom he would see alone—no other staff in adjoining offices, no secretaries, no receptionist. What if "something happened," like her accusing him of seduction? He realized that he had seen patients in the clinic when no one else had been around, but this was different—it was his own private office. And it was in his home. Once again, of course, these anxieties were not the patient's. Fortunately, the prereferral countertransference fears quickly abated as he engaged the patient in focusing together with him on her problems.

Her marriage was unsatisfactory, and she was suffering from bulimia, a condition that has been observed more and more recently. She was preoccupied with eating and shamefully regurgitating what she ate in order to maintain her figure. She wanted to be a "good" wife and "good" mother, and, most importantly of all, to be a good daughter to a mother with extravagant ambitions for her children. At that time in the therapist's own professional growth, he was caught up in attempting to emulate what he understood to be a psychoanalytic approach to such a problem and therefore embarked upon a three-times-a-week treatment methodology. His goal was to help this young woman gain insight into her relationships with her mother and her mother's ambitions for her through use of free association, development of and working through a transference neurosis, and uncovering unconscious impulses and conflicts. Thinking back about it twenty years later, the now experienced clinician realized that in the private practice situation he had been attempting to satisfy what he thought would be the demands of a psychoanalytic supervisor, the "illusory supervisor," even though he was in fact free from those demands.

With hindsight, the therapist believed that this patient would have been served better had he used different techniques based on psychoanalytic understanding but free from the attempt to respond to an "illusory supervisor's" demands. He might have confronted the patient more directly, as he would today, and he probably would have used many more active interventions. The practitioner is responsible for his own practice. In taking this responsibility, he may use theoretical constructs and guidelines applicable in many situations, but he will tailor them to suit the special needs of his individual patients.

The private practitioner shares the confusion that arises within all psychotherapists from the diversity of developmental and treatment theories extant combined with the dearth of powerful "scientific" proofs or even of specific "treatments" for specific disturbances. The more we know of various theoretical approaches to helping people, the more confused we may become. An advantage, as well as a disadvantage, of private practice is that being on one's own forces autonomous integration of at least some of the various approaches available. If a therapist has been trained in or had a great deal of experience primarily influenced by Freudian psychoanalytic theory and yet has been exposed to other theorists, he may be in conflict about how to proceed with his own individual patients. A colleague and a friend who has been heavily involved in a behavioral approach to psychotherapy reported recently that he found it impossible to function as a strict behaviorist in day-to-day practice privately because so many of the cases do not lend themselves to that particular approach. And a private practitioner who attempts to follow particular psychological dogma finds himself stymied and maybe even bewildered.

These observations lead to suggesting to the beginning private practitioner that he be ready to forsake any "religious" commitment to one particular theory and be prepared to meet the needs of his patients as they present themselves using whatever theoretical or methodological approaches he can familiarize himself with. The supervisor to whom he reports resides within himself. It is this internal monitor that must be relied upon. It has been observed that the most therapeutically successful practitioners are those who call upon many different theoretical ideas and are not narrowly bound to one particular theoretical orientation that is cast in concrete. Of course, the classical psychoanalyst might say that he's not interested in bringing about a cure—that he's only interested in "analyzing" or understanding the dynamics of the patient. The results of such understanding may or may not be therapeutic, but that is not his concern. Most psychotherapists are interested in this understanding but also seek to reduce their clients' pain and help them function better. Nevertheless, the practitioner must have some base from which to work, and there lies a dilemma. That is, to feel comfortable about what one is doing in practice, one needs to be able to relate to a body of theory and practice methodology as a guide. Further, to break out of the isolation of private practice and relate to other practitioners, one needs to talk the language of, and, to some extent be part of, some group within which one feels a sense of acceptance. Yet at the very same moment one needs to be responsive to varying patient needs. These needs may call for using techniques and using ideas that may be foreign to one's base group. The dilemma is that as a private practitioner one may feel that allegiance to a particular way of thinking may create tension when confronted with the immediate demands of an individual client that requires divergence from the theory which one has been taught to rely on. In an agency or a clinic where some particular school of thought prevails, one may abide by that particular prevailing idea and feel participant in it. In private practice, however, one is faced with a whole array of problems and of different kinds of clientele, and one must devise one's own way.

Many therapists find it difficult to admit to certain colleagues and peers that they are following procedures which do not meet the particular rules and regulations methodologically prescribed by some of their supervisors. The more experience one has and the more confident one is in one's autonomy, the more ready one may be to confess to variations from all sorts of methodological rules. Theories of therapy are not to be treated as religious dogma anyway. One caveat, however, is that while private practice offers the opportunity for devising one's own way of proceeding in a therapeutic encounter, it is nevertheless necessary to check against what the Freudian psychoanalysts call "wild analysis," or poorly thought-through idiosyncratic approaches to therapy. The danger in private practice is to become so isolated that one goes off in wild ways. The danger, of course, in a bureaucratically organized practice is to regress to a rote way of dealing with patients. Private practice requires a high degree of intellectual and emotional fortitude. One must take responsibility to follow in the literature new approaches, and to attend scientific meetings and institutes. But in the end the private practitioner must rely on his own judgment to distill what is useful and to apply it in his own individual practice.

By the way, when a therapist in private practice receives a referral, there is often a question as to how he should acknowledge the referring person. Generally, a brief note or telephone call is all that is required. The content of the note or telephone call simply consists of the facts of the referral: "So and so contacted me for help. Thank you." Unless there is some pressing reason to do so, no further reporting or consultation is required or expected. The referring person, the patient, and the recipient of the referral are apt to feel best about this limited response. And issues of confidentiality are simplified.

Observations of the behavior of therapists, especially in communities where one school of thought may be dominant, for example, psychoanalytic thought in the Chicago area, indicate that therapists who are members of one group, say the Institute for Psychoanalysis, tend largely to disregard the work of those who are involved in other groups, like the Adlerian institutes, and vice versa. A member of one or the other who describes or discusses the work of the alternate group often is regarded as suspect. A further observation from direct clinical appraisals of patients who previously have been in one or the other kind of treatments is that the individual therapists operated in their own unique ways but probably did not discuss their "deviations" with their colleagues. And certainly, what is written about a particular way of approaching therapy seems often a far cry from what actually happens in the clinical exchange between patient and therapist. In some ways, the process through which an individual practitioner develops his way of operating in the therapeutic situation is analogous to what various therapists, especially Margaret Mahler, have described of children's growth patterns in attaining individuality and independence. Mahler, having directly observed children's growth for more than 40 years, asserts that at certain points in the child's life he must introject and integrate both the good and the bad aspects of the mother and thus eventually learn how to tolerate ambivalence within himself, ultimately thereby gaining the capacity for autonomous living. So must the effective therapist integrate both the good and the bad aspects of various theoretical orientations and tolerate a great deal of ambivalence and ambiguity about these orientations.

The therapist, nevertheless, must present himself to the patient as having some solidly integrated sense of direction and hopefulness about the efficacy of his efforts. This problem exists for the therapist in an institution or clinic or agency, but it is most particularly present in the private practice situation. In the agency or clinic, the practitioner reports to others what he is doing. In the private practice situation, there is no one to whom to report. Unfortunately, in the area of treatment of emotional disturbances there are few specific guidelines for treatment. It differs from ordinary medical practice, where a certain symptomatology may lead to fairly specific diagnosis of a disease and reasonably widely accepted formulations of specific treatments for it.

Certainly there is a growing body of knowledge about specific emotional problems and specific interventions. But this body of knowledge is still far from complete, and the interventions are a good deal more vague. For example, in dealing with what is classified as a "borderline" child, there are times when one might recommend compulsive-obsessive behaviors as a means of helping the child to gain control over his internal impulses. On the other hand, were one confronted with a so-called "neurotic" child, one might discourage the use of obsessive-compulsive behavior. Unfortunately, to show the state of disarray within the field, there are some who do not even allow that there is such a thing as a "neurosis" for children or adults either (see the DSM III), so that the treatment modality for one or the other is at best vague. One can prescribe a specific medication for a kidney transplant patient and be ready to alter the prescription as new findings are reported. But a wide variety of "prescriptions" for a course of treatment for troubled children and adults exists. And while one may understand and have a good deal of scientific proof for a given illness's being derived from the presence of certain microbes, in the arena of emotional disturbance it is very difficult ever to isolate specific determinants for a specific emotional disturbance. As a consequence, a specific treatment approach for a given illness is rarely available. Given this state of affairs in the area of emotional disturbance, there continues to be the need for a highly individualized approach. To a very large extent, the treatment of every individual situation presented to the private practitioner is an experimental one.

The Faith of Counselors

Another kind of situation that one may confront, hopefully not immediately but only after one has been in practice a long time, will provide further illumination. A young woman presents herself. She is married, unsatisfactorily. Her husband is a poor wage earner. He is not interested in her sexually and makes himself unavailable emotionally. She herself is bright, feels inadequate, and indeed feels herself to be a very emotionally disturbed person. Her symptoms are excruciating, including feelings of depersonalization and sometimes of being a multiple personality. At times when she is particulary distraught, she will physically injure herself, including cutting into her own body with a knife "to get at where it hurts." It would be easy to label her psychotic or borderline. In the course of treatment she manages to separate herself from her husband, learns to drive, engages in a technical education program, and becomes self-supporting. The morbid and dangerous symptoms are abated. She nevertheless is subject to intense episodes of depression, sometimes suicidal, that seem unrelated to environmental or internally determined events. The therapist speculates—and one must underline *speculates*—that possibly there is an organic process that leads to her excruciating depressions and therefore refers her to a specialist in psychopharmacology.

The pharmacologist engages the patient in a series of drug trials. The patient responds sometimes with salutary results and sometimes with unconvincing results. The pharmacologically oriented psychiatrist *has faith* in his particular armamentarium of treatments. The dynamically oriented therapist *has faith*, with some doubts, in his armamentarium. The psychopharmacologist experiments with various medications, trying always to avoid discouragement on the part of the patient. The dynamically oriented therapist allows for the possibility of organic involvement and encourages the patient in her pursuit of medication that will help her avoid catastrophic depressions. Both the pharmacologically oriented psychiatrist and the dynamically oriented therapist *are hopeful* but are indeed experimenting in efforts to help the patient. Because the knowledge is limited, both are optimistic but neither is certain. Theoretically, the pharmacologically oriented psychiatrist believes that there are either chemical or possibly genetically determined organic causes for the patient's problems. The dynamically oriented therapist believes that the patient's problems are developmentally determined. Each may be somewhat skeptical of the other, but not completely convinced of the validity of their own theories. A combined approach is based on at least two very different theoretical explanations of the patient's behavior. Neither theoretical explanation has been scientifically thoroughly demonstrated. Both approaches progress from a *hopeful but unproven position*. Unfortunately, many emotional problems fall into this ambiguous pit, and both the dynamically oriented therapist and the pharmacological therapist continue to work for the benefit of the patient *partly on faith* rather than on thoroughly scientifically proven knowledge. The dynamically oriented psychotherapist, however, must always be aware that when he refers a patient to the pharmacologist, the patient may feel rejected, shunted off to someone else because the therapist doesn't want him any longer. The psychotherapist may even teach the pharmacologist something about this phenomenon. Certainly the psychotherapist must be alert to help the patient with such feelings as they arise—so should the pharmacologist.

Sometime in the early 1960s I presented a paper at a professional meeting. It was entitled, "See Me! Hear Me! Say My Name!"[33] The message conveyed was that the most important components of psychotherapy are to be able to see that patient for what he is; to hear what he says, listening with the "third ear"; and to "Say my name," meaning, "Recognize me. Acknowledge me as an unique individual. Help me to feel that I exist. Let me know that I am a Self. Through you, let me be affirmed." This is probably the essence of treatment of all patients, whatever their diagnostic categorization, and of all therapy approaches. Indeed, diagnosis is a means of expressing understanding and an aid to accepting the patient in the most profoundly meaningful way. A friend suggests that the Greek roots of the word "diagnosis" mean to "distinguish," to "discern," and that this is what every patient wants—that his differences from all others, his uniqueness, be observed and acknowledged. Diagnosis is an integral part of the treatment process. "Treatment" represents the setting of a stage or plat-form upon which the patient may stand with a growing firm-ness of footing while he struggles through the tangles of developmental chaos toward self-acknowledgment, self-con-trol, self-esteem. There probably are no "cures" of mental ill-ness or of emotional disturbances. Mental illness does exist. The illness may recede in prominence as emotional develop-ment in general is fostered, attained, and rewarded. But its presence will persist like a shadow in the background. Kohut believes that the heart of the therapeutic process is to repair early narcissistic defects and thus bring about cure. His con-tentions are yet to be proven. Emotional disturbances as distin-guished from illness seem generally to be a manifestation of a developmental thrust. The disturbance disappears as the de-velopment proceeds. Adolescents provide the most vivid and aggravating examples of this phenomenon. Most of what seems to count the most in therapy is the quality of the relationship with the therapist as experienced by the patient. It must pro-vide the nutrients for growth. The more the therapist is capable of understanding and then communicating that understanding to the patient and the more the therapist is able to accept the growing insights generated by his patients, the more they feel affirmed and confident of their capacity to grow. Perhaps this is not far different from an adequate mothering experience in early childhood.

Carl Jung may have said all this years ago and better. "Ex-perience has taught me to keep away from therapeutic 'meth-ods' as much as from diagnosis. The enormous variation among individuals and their neuroses has set before me the ideal of approaching each case with a minimum of prior assumptions. . . . In reality everything depends on the man and little or noth-ing on the method."[34] Hogan asserts that "although the litera-ture is replete with therapeutic recipes, very few attempts have been made to find out if they truly have any bearing on outcome."[35]

In his book *The Faith of Counselors*, Paul Halmos writes about definitions of the ideally well-trained psychoanalyst:

> Above all we can imagine him [the analyst] with a rounded-out personality enabling him to combine his knowledge with creative intuition, making him capable of empathy and of identifying himself easily with his patients, of being kindly without expecting anything in return, and of never feeling narcissistically wounded by certain developments in the treatment of his patients

He goes on to quote Charlotte Towle, the late great social work educator:

> Social work, by its very nature, needs workers who have considerable capacity to live beyond absorption in self and who are potentially creative. . . . The capacity is revealed in the educational process through liking and concern for people as individuals, which holds when they, in the midst of disadvantageous circumstances, are often least likeable. It is revealed in readiness, as knowledge and understanding is attained, to assume responsibility, to give understanding as well as services, to endure denial and frustration of unresponsive or hostile clients—in short, to give both mind and heart to the learning experience.[36]

Unfortunately, such paragons of virtue and nobility seem to be in short supply. Most of us fail to match these ideals. Perhaps the absolute requirement to be insisted on in any respectable therapist is the possession of a working sense of humor. Without it one is lost.

Three men who have suffered at the hands of therapists who apparently lost their humor and consequently not only failed their patients, but may even have injured them, serve as illustrations of what not to do in private practice. The first patient began "acting out" homosexually after his therapist suicided. The second broke away from his therapist after years of trying to do so because the therapist took him on as a homosexual lover during the treatment in spite of the patient's impulses and wishes to behave as a heterosexual. The third was sent for a series of shock treatments after he confessed to his therapist that all he wanted from treatment was to learn how to be a more successful homosexual.

In private practice, where the supports of a bureaucratic structure are largely absent, the uncertainties of theory and methodology in the mental health professions are felt most keenly. However, the mental health professional needs to remind himself that the medical profession and social scientists generally face similarly frustrating recognition of inability to control their special segments of human life. For example, political scientists have been unable to control events in such a way as to avoid wars and other kinds of political upheavals. Economists have been unable to control the economies of countries, let alone of the world, in such a way as to avoid depressions. Physicians obviously have been unable to control or to curb certain kinds of illnesses, such as cancer. All of those groups of scientists have been able to diagnose or to identify the nature of a particular illness and even post hoc to determine what might have been done to prevent or control it, but have not been able to prevent certain unfortunate occurrences or to bring about their "cure."

There is a major difference, however, between the situation of the political scientists or the economist and that of the psychotherapist in private practice. The difference is that the latter is directly confronted by an individual suffering from some particular disorder that causes great pain. And he is called upon to ameliorate or "cure" this condition individually.

It is often a great disappointment to both therapist and client alike to have to acknowledge that the therapist cannot cure. Working through that realization may constitute one of the most important components of psychotherapy. But it is hard.

The political scientist or the economist is called upon to relate to a class of disturbance for large numbers of people within an institutional structure. If and when he fails, there is no one person or small group of persons to whom he is accountable. The therapist in private practice is accountable directly to an individual or a small group or family. Psychotherapists have to be "emotionally involved" with each patient to some degree while simultaneously maintaining an "objective" distance. The stress of balancing between involvement and distance is probably the most wearing and burdensome aspect of practicing psychotherapy. And the private practitioner is without an immediately available institutional structure to support him. One way of coping with this kind of stress is by keeping an ongoing experimental view based on collecting data and comparing them with the theoretical constructs to which one has been exposed. And always the therapist must maintain a readiness to be amused by himself and the worlds to which his patients expose him.

Frieda Fromm-Reichman, in her gem of a book called *Principles of Intensive Psychotherapy*, recommended that the beginning practitioner have at least two cases to start with. The reasons that she offered were that if one case goes badly, the second will enable the practitioner to raise his spirits, and further, that having more than one case helps a practitioner to avoid become overinvolved with just one patient.[37]

Before concluding this discussion a comment should be made regarding the psychotherapist who leaves a clinic, hospital or social agency to enter into private practice and is interested in taking some of his clients with him. Some agencies as a matter of policy object to this practice, while others encourage it. Some object only if the practitioner is a psychologist or clinical social worker, but do not if the practitioner is a psychiatrist. The issue is complex. For the author, the guiding principles are: first, no client or patient is ever "owned" by an institution or by a therapist, and, second, the best interests of the client must be held paramount. Usually, clients prize continuity in therapeutic relationships and wish to follow their therapists into the private practice setting. Therapists may make special arrangements to charge less than usual fees in order to make it feasible for their clients. With the possible exception of the rare person who is incompetent to judge, clients profit from being encouraged to make their own choice as to whether to follow their therapist into private practice or to begin treatment with another therapist assigned within the institution. Institutional policies, in this author's view, ought to encourage rather than discourage such opportunities. And therapists ought to be supported to make such arrangements possible. The danger of a therapist exploiting his relationship with an institutional client to build his private practice is likely to be less than the potential damage to clients of having their treatment interrupted.

But practices, like everything else, have middles and endings too. One kind of ending is death. A livelier way of ending is to sell one's practice. Another way of ending would be to quietly or passively peter out of practice into retirement. It's more comfortable to discuss the middle of a practice, the mature practice. Beginnings are often exciting, but middle maturity can be mellowing. People in middle age would like to think that the worst tragedies are behind them, although their experience teaches otherwise. Perhaps there will always be the occasional 3 a.m. panic phone call, or the hysterical parent of a crazy obnoxious teenager who believes that therapy is doing more harm than good, or the irate spouse who has homicide in his heart. There will always be the patient who succumbs to an incurable illness and dies leaving the therapist to be therapeutic with the survivors while he himself is also mourning. The private practice of psychotherapy is always a tough business.

But when a practice is mature, one can select patients more carefully, and one may be able to balance his practice in a way that eases its burden and promotes its enjoyment. For example, there's nothing like a perky, cute adolescent girl, no matter how obnoxious her behavior in general, to liven an otherwise gray day. And there's great satisfaction and stimulation to be derived from work with a 70-plus feisty, crusty, gray-bearded curmudgeon fighting a bereavement depression. He is particularly welcome after a session with a 35-year-old middle-level executive ambivalent about whether he really wants to continue clawing his way up the hierarchical corporate ladder, especially since he's mad at his wife. Now of course there's very little a therapist can do about who is referred to him. But some choice is possible about which patients will be taken on when he knows that his hours are likely to be filled or fillable, and that his sources of referrals are stable and loyal. On the other hand, for better or worse, there is no way to know in advance where a patient is going to take one when a case begins. The "for better" part is that surprises are much more interesting than quite predictable courses. The "or worse" is that some surprises one might well do without. For example, any therapist would think twice about accepting the depressed young woman described earlier, who deferred telling her therapist the extent and depth of her pathology until they were so far into a relationship that it could not safely be discontinued. It is unnerving and wearing to confront details of life-threatening behavior like self-immolation. Nevertheless, it does get one's juices flowing.

The practitioner who has developed a mature private practice as a lifelong career is fortunate. It brings him a better than average income, gives him greater flexibility in using his time, and generates a deep sense of satisfaction in being able to help others live more useful and fulfilling lives. Only the arrogant and less than honest would assert, however, that he never experienced doubts, failures, and a desire to do something else with his life.

Probably the most painful experiences in a private practice are the instances where a patient's suicide attempt succeeds. It is doubtful often that suicide can be prevented, but the possibility persists and is troublesome. When it occurs, even the most experienced ought to engage in postmortem explorations with consultants to come to a better understanding of what happened. It is a way not only to ease one's mind, but to be prepared to do things differently if ever a similar situation arises again.

One of the more frustrating experiences in a practice is to be sued for malpractice, especially if it's a nuisance suit. Most therapists need not be overly concerned about the possibilities of being sued for malpractice if they follow two important rules: (1) they have reasonable malpractice insurance, and (2) they strive to maintain the highest ethical standards possible in their work. Wise therapists subscribe strongly to the ancient Hippocratic doctrine "non nocere," or "do no harm." If one is confused about a case, seek consultation or discuss it with the patient. Awareness that one can do harm either by doing something or by doing nothing is necessary.

In a recently completed review of 300 malpractice suits brought against psychiatrists, psychologists, or clinical social workers, it was startling to learn how few of these suits were won by the consumer, even in instances of what appeared to be grossly unethical or negligent behavior.[38] One may take a little comfort from these findings, but one would continue to urge all psychotherapists to conduct their practice within the parameters of ethical and professional standards, meaning mostly to maintain the interests of the patient above all else. Internal monitors are far more effective and demanding for mature psychotherapists than are external forces.

Behaviors to Be Avoided

Since the thrust of this book has been on the positive, it is something of a departure to list negative behaviors to be avoided by practitioners. The more obvious are (1) sexual acting out with patients; (2) failure to clarify policies regarding fees early in the contact; (3) raising fees without adequate notice and discussion in a timely fashion; (4) failure to protect a

patient's confidentiality even inadvertently, and especially
with other professionals; (5) failure to take responsibility for
one's own limitations, gaps in knowledge, lack of understanding, and especially projecting any or all of these deficits onto
the patient—blaming the patient for lack of progress. There
are probably many others that could be listed. Indeed a book
could be written about what not to do.

Anticipating the Unexpected

Anyone who spends a lifetime in private practice is likely
to experience many confusing, upsetting, and downright immo-
bilizing situations, along with delightful soul-enriching opportunities.

Some examples of the enriching opportunities are to treat
the adult children and grandchildren of former clients. Or, at
the other end of the life cycle, to have older adult clients refer
their aging parents. Another is to use hypnotherapy to aid a colleague's concert-pianist client overcome a performance block.
Satisfying when all goes well, but problematic overall is the
chance to treat members of a colleague's family. To use all
your personal resources to avert the hospitalization of a client,
particularly a young one, successfully is a special therapeutic
triumph.

On the other hand, facing clients after you have undergone a widely publicized personal calamity demands enduring
strength beyond anything you might have anticipated. Or being
called upon to treat the patients of your own therapist after he
has suicided will tax your deepest reserves. A problem that be-
sets any long-experienced, well-known therapist is to find an
appropriate person to treat members of his own family without
unduly burdening the therapeutic process with his presence,
seen or unseen. Or, if one is highly respected within the profes-

sional community as a standard-setting leader, teacher, consultant, it is often complicated to make a referral to a colleague without placing a special burden of implied expectations for success upon the other therapist. The other side of that equation is to accept a referral from a therapist whom one supervises, with exaggerated expectations possible on the part of one or both.

There are, too, the exceptional situations which occur, like the referral of a patient who turns out to be the the failed client of the therapist spouse of one's own therapist. Then there are the instances where a client overpays his fee, or makes the therapist beneficiary of a life insurance policy. The client who refuses to pay presents another kind of problem. A frequently encountered situation, particularly in smaller communities, is that of meeting clients socially or in political or activity groups that engender close and prolonged contact. Another instance that may constitute a special message is when another professional, like a physician, lawyer, or clergyman, suddenly initiates an unusual number of referrals. The spate of referrals may actually constitute a "cry for help" for himself. And finding a way to respond tactfully but effectively is difficult. While this is hardly a laundry list of the kinds of things one may meet in a long-term practice, let us look at some of them in a little greater depth to gain a bit of the flavor of what it's like to be in private practice.

Recently an amusing story circulated about a prominent long experienced psychoanalyst who referred his patients to a dentist friend for support whenever the analyst was away on vacation or at meetings. When asked why he chose a dentist rather than another analyst, the analyst replied that he knew of no other colleagues whom he could trust. Of course, some of us speculated that a more compelling reason for the choice is that he feared that another colleague might discover possible inadequacies he otherwise concealed behind his consulting room doors. Indeed, even the most experienced, respected, and successful psychotherapists experience discomfort at the prospect of other peers overseeing their work directly, or seeing themselves exposed through the direct revelations of a close relative or a former patient to a colleague. Nevertheless, most of us learn to cope with the stress of exposure reasonably well. After all, our clients eventually bare our foibles to us anyway no matter how adroitly we may try to conceal them.

A more difficult situation is where we need to refer a close relative to a colleague who may hold an exaggeratedly exalted opinion of us, and may therefore feel constrained to do a super therapy job since we will be watching. A young clinical social worker with relatively little professional experience was surprised when the director of a prestigious therapy training center referred his own son to the social worker for treatment instead of choosing one of his own colleagues or even one of his students or graduates. As it turned out, the director was fearful not so much of possible revelations about himself, but of the possible negative consequences for his son of unresolved countertransference feelings of therapists too closely associated with the director.

Another related kind of experience is the following. A woman was referred who had been in treatment for a long time with another therapist. Unresolved transference phenomena prevented the patient from returning to this therapist. Treatment with the new therapist began before the second therapist asked specifically for the name of the previous therapist. The previous therapist turned out to be the spouse of the new therapist's own personal therapist. This revelation of an almost incestuous therapeutic entanglement presented a number of ethical and technical problems for the second therapist. First, he preferred not to share with his patient who his own therapist was. Second, he felt it would be a betrayal of his patient to reveal the situation to his own therapist. However, in his own examination of himself, the second therapist became aware that he enjoyed keeping this "dirty little secret" from his own therapist. To help himself to minimize the possible inadvertent negative effects of the circumstances of his patient, this therapist sought consultation with another colleague. Long after the treatment ended, the second therapist reported that all worked out reasonably well. Perhaps the moral of this vignette is that it is best to secure certain factual information before agreeing to undertake treatment of a new patient.

Since therapy is a complex business at best, most of us try to minimize extraneous complications whenever possible. That is why in most instances therapists won't accept their own close friends or relatives as clients. Most will not accept relatives, close friends or associates of their current clients either, but will refer them to others. This practice may not seem consistent with the fact discussed earlier that one of the most important sources of referrals are clients, unless one assumes that it is only former clients who have successfully terminated treatment who make the referrals. This does not seem to be the case for the experienced therapists who have been in practice a long time.

Indeed, when one has been in practice long enough one may have the chance to treat the children or even the grandchildren of former clients. There are, of course, advantages and disadvantages to such opportunities, but the pluses seem to outweigh the minuses. For example, levels of trust are likely to be established much more rapidly. And although a therapist's memory of the significant aspects of a treatment conducted years earlier may not be intact or reliable, some traces may be of current value.

The longer a therapist continues in practice, the greater the likelihood that those vicissitudes of life of which Freud spoke so often will occur in the therapist's own life. A colleague who suffered the loss of his spouse in a tragic accident that was well publicized in the media had somehow to deal with his own and his patients' reactions when he resumed his practice. He took more than a month for his own private grieving before he reentered his office. Colleagues had seen his clients during that interim to sustain them temporarily. Upon his return, he accepted their condolences and invited them to speak of the events and to ask questions freely. In this way he helped the clients to express their fears, guilt, and other reactions, including the mixture of feelings about inadvertently invading the therapist's privacy. The therapist, too, was helped to work through his own mourning by facing it with his patients. He reported, however, that the toughest confrontations were with children in his practice whose deepest fears about their own helplessness, destruction and destructiveness were stimulated and expressed in raw nakedness. Some children, for example, wanted to know exactly what happens to you after you're dead and in a grave and become a skeleton. Somehow, the bromides or other conventional responses that one makes at times of bereavement were not enough, according to this colleague, for these very much upset children. Once again, this therapist in his pain demonstrated that the best interests of his clients required facing their fears along with his own head on.

There are other situations one confronts in a mature practice that require intense attention and responsiveness. Two of these are the instances where a client significantly overpays his fees, or makes the therapist beneficiary of a life insurance policy. Each of these may be an ominous message or an attempt to manipulate the therapist. The message may be, "I intend to kill myself. You'll miss me when I'm gone. You won't be able to forget me because you'll have my money." Obviously, the therapist can't erase the insurance policy, and may not even be able to return the excess fees. What the therapist can do, however, is insist on focusing on the meaning of the patient's behavior, and even ultimately to consider with the patient the possible necessity to terminate treatment. However, even this alternative must be dealt with carefully lest it be improperly interpreted as the rejection that the patient has been anticipating all along: "You won't accept my money. You won't accept me!" When such behavior persists in the face of the therapist's continuing efforts to help the patient work on it, consultation with a colleague may be called for perhaps to uncover something that is not adequately understood.

Another more pleasant instance is that of one therapist, secure in his mature practice, who makes use of a second therapist who has a subspecialty of hypnotherapy to help with an unusually persistent problem. Specifically, the first therapist has been treating a patient with multiple problems. The patient is a concert pianist and during the course of his treatment he develops a block against performing publicly. The hypnotherapist is called upon to intervene. He uses relatively simple hypnotic techniques including rehearsal of the circumstances of the concert while under hypnosis in addition to some general post-hypnotic suggestions. The procedure is effective, the patient performs his concert and continues in treatment with his therapist. Everyone does not necessarily live happily ever after, but the secure therapist is grateful to the hypnotherapist as is the patient and the regular treatment proceeds even more fruitfully than before.

A less happy circumstance reported by another therapist occurred when his former analyst suicided. One of the analyst's patients sought out this particular therapist, unaware of the therapist's relationship with the analyst. The therapist decided against revealing his relationship to the deceased because he thought it would complicate matters for the patient. In a sense they were both patients. The contact was successfully carried out and ultimately terminated. This example illustrates the reality that the role of therapist is interchangeable with that of patient but that it is vitally important to understand the therapeutic role with all its expectations and special rules which must be adhered to assiduously if the identified patient is to profit from the relationship.

Often in private practice one is presented with an especially decompensated person like an adolescent who is suffering from an acute depression or an anxiety state. Although it might be more convenient, comfortable and safer to hospitalize such a person, many practitioners prefer to work intensively with him, perhaps seven days a week for several weeks, possibly employing medication as an adjunct, until the acute episode subsides. Young and old prefer to avoid the stigmatizing and often demoralizing impact of hospitalization. Private practitioners may be in a better position to make the kind of investment and the necessary adjustments to carry out this kind of function than institution-based therapists.

Finally, experienced private practitioners have noted that certain professionals in the community from time to time make a flurry of referrals. Often, that is a message that the professional making the referrals is indirectly asking for contact and help himself. The alert therapist responds in order to ascertain whether or not the message is indeed what he thinks it may be. People in the helping professions often suffer great stress and find it difficult to turn to others for help. This is especially true in smaller tight-knit communities. The private practitioner may be in a position discreetly to make himself available to help such people in his community.

Since each therapist's practice is unique just as his clients are unique, the list of situations that may be encountered is endless. The examples I've offered may provide a bit of flavor of what private practice is like.

The private practice of psychotherapy is at once intensely interesting and satisying and also intensely demanding emotionally and intellectually. On balance, it's a good place to be.

In the final chapter that follows, there will be a summation and a consideration of several last issues.

CHAPTER 9

Private Practice Today and Tomorrow

And in conclusion . . .

T HE PRACTICE OF PSYCHOTHERAPY as a professional activity has flourished and grown especially during the past 40 to 50 years. Criticisms have been leveled at its practice, of course, from the beginning. Psychotherapists have been accused of being exploitive charlatans. They have been credited with great power which they have been accused of using to undermine the moral fiber of communities and even of nations by mollycoddling the weak, the immoral, and the otherwise undesirable and promoting degenerative, loose sexual and other moral and ethical values. Some argue that investing energy, money, manpower, and interest in trying to solve man's problems by tackling them one by one deflects from the "more appropriate," "more effective" emphasis on larger economic, social, and political activities.

One may be sympathetic to these arguments without agreeing with them. It is probably true that psychotherapy has impacted on society in directing us all toward attitudes of greater permissiveness and greater understanding of human motives at levels deeper than the simple or superficial. Psychotherapy is intolerant of shibboleth, demands high levels of honesty and integrity from its practitioners and its consumers, and insists on supporting the dignity of all men. It makes an implicit demand on all of society for greater straightforwardness, less pretense. Maybe it can only be practiced within a society that permits free expression by individuals.

Generally, the values and ethics of psychotherapy are stronger and better developed than its scientific theories and methodologies. Here lies its greatest vulnerability to criticism, but also its greatest opportunity for the future. Sometime, perhaps during the next 25 years, clearer, more specific, better-pinpointed knowledge of human development will evolve so that therapists will have deeper understanding of how things go wrong and how to help set them right. Whether the future of psychotherapy will rest in the sciences or will move toward the humanistic, clinically philosophic or will continue to occupy a space somewhere between remains an open question. The safest bet is probably with the third possibility. A certainty is that the demand for psychotherapy will continue and will even increase.

For every patient in therapy there are at least one to four or more others who are somehow affected by any changes that are forthcoming. As many as 100 million Americans may in some way be touched by psychotherapy at the present time. Yet many professionals worry that psychotherapy has failed to develop a readily transmitted body of cumulated knowledge that can ensure the competence of its average practitioner. Orne (1975) points out that "unfortunately, the basic science that underlies psychotherapy remains to be developed."[39] Frank (1975), on the other hand, asserts that the diversity of both psychotherapies and the conditions that respond to them is more apparent than real.[40] Basch (1980) attempts to reconcile his psychoanalytic, psychodynamic approach with differing methods and theories. He says, "Rather than choosing among various therapies, I should like to suggest that we therapists can learn from one another's variations in emphasis to pay attention to factors we might otherwise overlook. Our differences are more in language than in practice. . . .[41]

Perlman (1970) reminds us that "typically caseworkers do not treat neurotic or psychotic (pre- or present or post-) conditions. *They treat people who have such conditions.* The people who have them are not the same as their sickness."[42] Germain (1970) says, "A modern scientific orientation supports attitudes favoring multiple bases for defining problems, a variety of helping modes, and an array of realistic objectives which pose tasks not only for the worker but for the client. . . . If one is too strongly attached to one's preconceived model, one will of necessity miss all radical discoveries. It is amazing to what degree one may fail to register mentally an observation which does not fit the initial image. On the other hand, if one is too open-minded and pursues every hitherto unknown phenomenon, one is almost certain to lose one's self in trivia."[43] All in all, while psychotherapy appears still to be struggling to achieve a "science of psychotherapy," it seems essential that we maintain a mind open to new ideas and concepts while using what has already been learned to build upon. We do stand on the shoulders of Sigmund and Anna Freud, Spitz, Erikson, Watson, Sullivan, Skinner, Perlman, Towle, Richmond, and many others. The knowledge accumulates, although the certainty about which among many methodologies to choose in order to help a variety of patient groups grows more slowly. The optimist who says the glass is "half full" may rely on the hope that experience based on experimentation will increase our certainty in selection. The pessimist who perceives the glass as "half empty" may predict gloom and doom for our efforts. The optimists are certainly more appealing.

The faith of patients coupled with the faith of counselors is probably central to what makes therapy work at all. Sometimes, the patient's discovery that someone has enough faith in him to want to help is in itself a powerful boost to morale.

Sometimes, the therapist's faith in his theories and conceptual schema sustains his own interest in the patient and reassures him as to the validity of his procedures in the face of therapeutic failures. A great deal is expected and demanded of therapists.

Private practice is a valuable modality through which to deliver psychotherapy services to people who need them. Indeed, many professionals who respect community service agencies nevertheless regard the private practice model as a superior service delivery mechanism. In private practice, the therapist is accountable first to the patient or consumer, second to the profession, and third to the public or the community at large. Private practice is superior to institutional practice with respect to placing first priority on accountability to the consumer. Autonomy, or self-determination, is one of the basic principles of all democratic political and social philosophy, not to mention theories of psychological development. To exercise autonomy, one has to be able to choose—or perhaps, as some cynics suggest, one has to have the "illusion of choice." The difference between going to a clinic and going to a private practitioner is like the difference between having a benevolent parent decide what is "best" for one and deciding one's self whom to turn to for help. Too many agencies and institutions violate the basic principle of client autonomy. For example, the consumer's need to feel a sense of continuity in his relationship to the person in whom he struggles to invest trust must be recognized as of first importance (even in this age of "future shock") by any professional who offers help. Yet how many "helping" institutions make continuity of treatment with a specific therapist a first-priority matter? Unfortunately, the very system of institutional structure works against this elementary necessity for the client. In private practice a mutually acceptable contract between two or more people is agreed upon with quid pro quo expectations. This arrangement minimizes for the patient the demeaning aspects of having to seek help. And it helps to minimize negative countertransference reactions on the part of the helper.

The subjective experiences of many therapists upon entering into private practice are these paradoxical reactions: first, pleasure at the freedom of carrying the full burden of responsibility for their performance with the client, and second, a sobering realization of how hard they feel they must work in order to justify the financial burden placed upon the client and the heavy emotional investment he makes. One therapist reported that one of his clients, whom he had formerly seen in a clinic, had to reassure him that he need not "try so hard," that the client had the same faith in the practitioner as he had had before.

There are, of course, arguments against private practice and in favor of institutional service. One of these is an economic argument, and another has to do with accountability. It is argued that in private practice, especially where third-party payers subsidize the cost of treatment, there may be a tendency to exploit either the patient or the third-party payer or both, and that inordinate sums of money may pour into a relatively "nonproductive" segment of the economy. This is not the place to debate the general economic issues, but some have observed the relative economic efficiency of a practitioner in private practice versus agency practice and concluded that private practice is more efficient. For example, it is not unusual in psychiatric clinics or other institutions employing psychotherapists for the average productivity of each full-time staff member as measured in units of interviews held to be 20 per week for approximately 44 weeks, or 880 interviews per year. The cost per interview to the clinic, including overhead and community activities, is likely to be over $60 per visit for a gross cost per worker of $52,800. A private practitioner in full-time practice who charges $55/visit and holds 1,700 interviews (40 per week times 44 weeks) will earn a total gross of $93,500, but will hold twice the number of interviews at a lower cost per visit.

The private practice model seems more efficient. Naturally, this kind of comparison is somewhat simplistic in that it does not take into account factors in the clinic that inflate costs, nor does it account for the heavier work schedule of the private practitioner. Nevertheless, assertions about which model is more cost-effective should be based on careful study, not prejudice.

In regard to accountability or monitoring, there does seem to be an advantage to the institutional model where practice staff are supervised. However, demonstrations of how institutional monitoring of practice is effective in containing costs or improving quality of service remain to be made. The question of public monitoring of private practice will probably not be resolved by increasing use of professional peer standards review organizations, but that will be a small step in the proper direction. Nevertheless, many of us believe that the best controls on private practice are those exercised directly by the consumer in his right to discontinue and seek help elsewhere if he feels dissatisfied.

Another set of problems that is of special concern to the social health planners is that of guaranteeing equal access to service for all the population. This concern focuses on the existence of community services for all and the availability of adequate personnel to staff them. Social planners fear that private practice will siphon off the best therapists, whatever their particular profession, leaving few to man the public facilities. Knesper and Carlson (1981) found that 55 percent of 900 psychiatrists who graduated between 1961 and 1976 were in the private rather than public sector. They conclude:

> Some may feel that psychiatry is blemished because so many psychiatrists flee public-sector practice; we think psychiatry has few apologies to make. Not wishing to compromise standards of quality care by working in State Mental Hospitals or other organizations, which have long been criticized as providing second or third rate and sometimes abusive care, hardly seems the subject

for apology. Psychiatry, and the rest of medicine, government, educational institutions and numerous others share in the failure to develop mental health care provision systems with sufficient resources to provide quality care to the severely and chronically mentally ill. . . .[44]

This refusal to apologize seems to constitute a belligerent apology. Yet there is considerable doubt that if opportunities for private practice suddenly shrank or dried up, the staffing conditions in public institutions would rapidly or markedly improve. Currently, as the public and private job market for mental health professionals is shrinking in the face of federal and state budget containment, more potential staff are available, but few can find their way into public institutions. Some, no doubt, will turn to private practice as an alternative. But it will probably be a rejection by institutions more than a pulling in by private practice that will account for the movement, despite the aid of this book.

Arguments regarding the effects of the method of payment on the substance of treatment itself have long raged. The most comprehensive review is compiled in *The Effect of the Method of Payment on Mental Health Care Practice* (1975).[45]

Briefly, the issues boil down to the following: all who need help should be able to get it without spending more than they can afford; all socioeconomic strata of the population should have high-quality service available—avoiding a qualitatively differentiated multitiered delivery system; therapist and consumer ought to have a voice in determining the treatment relationship without fear that the choice is based on financial considerations rather than on clinical indications; therapists should be compensated adequately to provide incentive to do effective work without feeling tempted to exploit patients or to neglect them because payment is guaranteed; confidentiality of the treatment relationship should be protected; the kind of treatment and its duration should be chosen on the basis of clinical considerations rather than budget; what is best for society and for those who need care rather than for the individual therapist ought to guide practice; the loyalty and allegiance of the therapist should rest primarily with his patient, rather than with funders; any payment system will have an effect on the intimate treatment relationship, and the therapist must be able to deal with these effects openly without having to justify or protect his own or his employer's financial interests; economic issues ought not to monopolize the attention of organizations of mental health professionals; payment systems should not encourage organizational and legal conflicts between therapists from different professional disciplines.

Since there is little in life or in society that is perfect, it is no surprise to the ordinary observer that the "oughts" and "shoulds" listed above are often notable by their absence in the real life of psychotherapy practiced privately or in institutions. Some of us would say that there are fewer obstacles in private practice to realizing these ideals, but we would not be able forthrightly to assert that the needs of the underprivileged are being well served in private practice, or that there are no abuses of third-party funding mechanisms, or that all decisions regarding treatment are clinically determined rather than financially motivated. On the other hand, not all the most virtuous institution-based practices would escape similar or other criticisms. Perhaps an old-time minister's homily applies here: Let us acknowledge that we cannot prevent sin, but let us try our hardest to inhibit its enjoyment!

The Group for the Advancement of Psychiatry set down four major principles to guide improvement in mental health care delivery:

1. *Professional autonomy.* This does not mean professional license and the public be damned. It does mean the freedom to preserve confidentiality, to encourage the mutuality of choice between clinician and patient, and to monitor therapeutic performance and professional standards with the aim of improving performance rather than keeping down costs.

2. *Equity of care for all.* The polarities of adequate care for those who can pay a fee and inferior care for those who can't, and of one type of treatment for "good" acute patients and another for chronic patients, need to be narrowed. Therapists in institutional or private practice must do more than recite pious platitudes to the effect that quality of care for the poor must be upgraded. What we must or will be able to do probably resides in the area of political and social action.

3. *Personalization of treatment.* Fee-for-service practice encourages and is an incentive to abiding commitment to patients' needs. Similar incentive must be built into institutional care giving. Recipients of care must be treated as individuals, not as units.

4. *Diversity of mental health care mechanisms.* In the absence of any one certified, universally effective method of treatment, a variety of modalities permitting emphasis on various dimensions of treatment for individual, group, family, and society needs to be encouraged. A diversity of systems will also supply data for determining the relative effectiveness of different methods of treatment. These data can narrow significantly the polarization of medical and nonmedical approaches, which need to be allowed to operate without being forced to conform by financial or other constraints to one inflexible model.[46]

Once again, this set of principles, like the Ten Commandments, is advanced to guide behavior in the face of less than perfect practice. As with any other projected guidelines, it will take consistent and long-range effort on the part of all the therapeutic professionals, their organizations, and their allies to bring these principles to operational function. Among the most serious obstacles to their achievement are the rivalries between the several professions and the discord that exists within each of the professions.

Probably the most significant conflicts between the professions have their source in economic, status, and power considerations. These conflicts often referred to as "turf" or "guild"

issues, are mostly between medical and nonmedical professions. To a lesser extent, issues of "protection of the consumer
public" from less than fully competent psychotherapists are
also raised. Fortunately or unfortunately, there is no clear evidence to demonstrate that medical training is necessary or that
it guarantees competence in the practice of psychotherap.
Orne, Frank, and Basch, cited above, along with many others
testify to this reality.

In all probability, the interprofessional rivalries will continue to rage on the economic and political lobbying front for
some time to come. Hopefully, however, professionals of the
several disciplines will continue their work together and with
their patients, learning, failing, succeeding, and sharing what
they may have gleaned from the searing heat of one of the most
demanding kinds of work practiced by any professionals. The
adversities visited upon all mental health and helping professions by federal and state cutbacks in funding may have the
salutary political effect of driving the several professions—or
rather the organizations that represent them—into each other's arms in mutual defense actions. With a great deal of luck,
then, collaboration politically may lead to longer-range and far-
ther-reaching cooperation. Certainly Pollyanna would have it
so, and maybe just this time she could be right.

Another obstacle to progress within the mental health
field is internal opposition within each of the professions
toward private practice and often toward individualized psychotherapy altogether. Dynamically or psychoanalytically oriented medically trained psychiatrists are often looked upon by
their pharmacologically oriented colleagues as not practicing
medicine at all or, worse, as being charlatans. Clinical psychologists in private practice are often perceived by their academic
colleagues as having deserted the arena of pure science for the
hurly-burly world of the market place. And clinical social workers in private practice are often accused by their colleagues as
lacking concern for dealing with social problems, both because

they focus on one-to-one practice and because they are practicing outside an institutional aegis. Of course, as one wag insightfully puts it, "In unanimity there is cowardice and uncritical thinking." Perhaps the disagreements within each of the professions as well as those between them are antidotes to the pitfalls of unanimity, provided that the conflict remains within livable parameters and does not escalate to mutual or unilateral destruction.

In this book, the professions of psychiatry, psychology, and clinical social work have been treated interchangeably with respect to the private practice of psychotherapy. This is not to deny that there are distinctions among them or to overemphasize their overlapping functions in a "common village green." The intent has been throughout to present the entrepreneurial aspects of private practice within the framework of high standards of professional practice, competence, and ethical value systems. The "business" of private practice together with the technical "substance" of psychotherapeutic practice are interwoven, hopefully, in a creative way.

As one who has had a special interest in the impact that their careers have on people, this author has expressed his belief that a lifetime spent in a career as a psychotherapist, particularly in private practice, is a most desirable and salubrious undertaking for himself and for society. He may be a less than "saintly" entrepreneur, but he is certainly engaged in a noble work.

The future may see the creation of a wide variety of models of psychotherapy, of professions engaged in it, and of organizational structures to provide it. Chains of franchised therapy centers with "brand name" quality connotations may be set up employing different kinds of therapists and providing wide arrays of methodologies. Perhaps psychotherapy will emerge as the "fifth profession." Certainly demand for treatment will grow, and knowledge and skill will increase. Wouldn't it be delightful to be here 50 years hence to enjoy the progress made by then that will be built upon the base already constructed! To those readers who, like the author, will not have that opportunity, be of good cheer in the knowledge that our past struggles will have meaning beyond what we can possibly imagine.

Notes

1. F. E. Fiedler, "The Concept of an Ideal Therapeutic Relationship," *Journal of Consulting Psychology,* Vol. 14, pp. 239–245, 1950, and "A Comparison of Therapeutic Relationships: Psychoanalytic, Non-directive, and Adlerian Therapy," *Journal of Consulting Psychology,* Vol. 14, pp. 436–445, 1950. "The definition of the ideal relationship posited by experts in the field was very similar to any good interpersonal relationship." Fiedler found that experienced therapists could not be distinguished on the basis of their techniques, although experienced therapists did resemble the ideal more than inexperienced therapists.

2. Daniel J. Levinson, *The Seasons of a Man's Life,* Knopf, New York, 1978, p. 191.

3. Ruth Fizdale, "Formalizing the Relationship Between Private Practitioners and Social Agencies," *Social Casework,* December 1959; also, Alice D. Taggart, Sidney J. Berkowitz, and Sonya Penn, *Fee Charging in a Family Agency, Family Service Association of America,* New York, 1944; Sidney Berkowitz, "Reactions of Clients and Caseworkers Toward Fees," *Family Journal of Social Casework,* XXVII:4 (April 1947); Frances Levenson Beatman, "Interpretation of Agency Policy to Workers, Clients, Agency

Board and Community," presented at National Conference on Social Welfare, May 15, 1951; Celia Brody, "Fee Charging: A Dynamic in the Casework Process," *Family Journal of Social Casework*, XXX:2 (February 1949); Marjorie Boggs, "The Administrative and Casework Aspects of Fee Charging," *Family Journal of Social Casework*, XXX:8 (October 1949); Tina Clare Jacobs, "Attitudes of Social Workers Toward Fees," *Social Casework*, XXXIII:5 (May 1952); Frederika Neumann, "Administrative and Community Implications of Fee Charging," *Social Casework*, XXXIII:7 (July 1952).

4. Robert P. Quinn, Graham L. Staines, and Margaret R. McCullough, *Job Satisfaction: Is There a Trend?* Manpower Research Monograph No. 30, U. S. Department of Labor, Washington, D.C., 1974.

5. Arnold M. Levin, "Social Workers in Mid-Career," unpublished doctoral dissertation, University of Chicago, August 1976.

6. Levinson, Ibid., p. 60.

7. Bernice L. Neugarten, *Middle Age and Aging*, University of Chicago Press, Chicago, 1968; Bernice L. Neugarten, and Nancy Datan, "The Middle Years," in *American Handbook of Psychiatry*, Second Edition, edited by Silvano Arieti, Basic Books, New York, 1974.

8. Ibid.

9. W. E. Henry, and J. Sims, *The Fifth Profession: Becoming a Psychotherapist*, Jossey-Bass, San Francisco, 1971.

10. Arnold M. Levin (Ed.), *Handbook on the Private Practice of Social Work*, revised, NASW, Washington, D.C., 1974, p. 15.

11. Herman Borenzweig, "Agency Versus Private Practice: Similarities and Differences," *Social Work*, May 1981, pp. 241–242, NASW, Washington, D.C.

12. Ibid., p. 242.

13. Arnold M. Levin, "Private Practice Is Alive and Well," *Social Work*, vol. 21, no. 5, p. 359, September 1976.

14. Levin, "Social Workers in Mid-Career."

15. Dava Sobel, *New York Times Magazine*, Oct. 26, 1980, p. 29.

16. Ibid. Quote from Dr. Toksoz Byrom Karasu, Director, Department of Psychiatry, Bronx Municipal Hospital Center, Albert Einstein College of Medicine.

17. W. E. Henry, and J. Sims, *The Fifth Profession.*

18. Sigmund Freud, as quoted by Dava Sobel in *New York Times Magazine,* Oct. 26, 1980, p. 29.

19. V. C. Raimy (Ed.), *Training in Clinical Psychotherapy,* Prentice Hall, Englewood Cliffs, N.J., 1950, p. 93.

20. Tax Court ruling under Section 1.162-5(a)1 of the Income Tax Regulations. *Reports of the U.S. Tax Court,* Vol. 74, U.S. Government Printing Office, Washington, D.C., 1980, pp. 82–85.

21. Jerome Frank, "General Psychotherapy: The Restoration of Morale," in *American Handbook of Psychiatry,* Second Edition, Silvano Arieti, Editor-in-Chief, Vol. 5, Daniel X. Freedman and J. Dyrud, Editors, Basic Books, New York, 1975, pp. 184–185.

22. Daniel B. Hogan, *The Regulation of Psychotherapists,* Ballinger, Cambridge, Mass., 1979—particularly Vol. 2, *A Handbook of State Licensure Laws.*

23. Andrew Hacker, "The Shame of Professional Schools," *Harper's,* Oct. 1981, pp. 22–28.

24. *Webster's Unabridged Dictionary,* Second Edition, Springfield, Mass., 1958, p. 539.

25. Marquis Wallace, "Autonomy in Private Practice," unpublished Ph. D. dissertation, University of Chicago, 1977, p. 81.

26. Wallace, ibid., p. 62.

27. *Wall Street Journal,* Sept. 29, 1981, p. 1.

28. "Guide to Private Practice"(A special compilation, looseleaf, including many excerpts from regular newsletter), *Psychotherapy Finances,* Ridgewood Financial Institute, Inc., 75 Oak Street, Ridgewood, N.J., 1980, pp. 4–17.

29. Levin, *Handbook on the Private Practice of Social Work,* p. 25.

30. Ibid., p. 20.

31. Wallace, "Autonomy," p. 62.

32. Steven G. Weinrach, "Part Time Private Practice for the Reluctant Entrepreneur," *The Counseling Psychologist,* vol. 9, no. 1, pp. 87–89.

33. Arnold M. Levin, "See Me! Hear Me! Say My Name!" Unpublished paper.

34. C. G. Jung, *Psychological Reflections: A New Anthology of His Writings, 1905–1961,* selected and edited by J. Jacobi with R. F. C. Hull, Princeton University Press, Princeton, N.J., 1970, pp. 81–82.

35. Hogan, *The Regulation of Psychotherapists*, pp. 107–108.
36. Paul Halmos, *The Faith of Counselors*, Schocken Books, New York, 1966, pp. 182–183.
37. Frieda Fromm-Reichmann, *Principles of Intensive Psychotherapy*, University of Chicago Press, Chicago, 1950.
38. Hogan, ibid.
39. Martin Orne, "Psychotherapy in Contemporary America: Its Development and Context," in *American Handbook of Psychiatry*, Second Edition, Sylvano Arieti, Editor-in-Chief, vol. 5, Basic Books, New York, 1975, p. 4.
40. Jerome Frank, ibid., p. 120.
41. Michael Frans Basch, *Doing Psychotherapy*, Basic Books, New York, 1980, pp. 179–180.
42. Helen Harris Perlman, "The Problem Solving Model in Social Casework," in *Theories of Social Casework*, edited by Robert W. Roberts and Robert H. Knee, University of Chicago Press, Chicago, 1970, p. 167.
43. Carel Germain, ibid., p. 30.
44. M. D. Knesper and Bruce W. Carlson, "An Analysis of the Movement to Private Psychiatric Practice," *Archives of General Psychiatry*, vol. 38, Aug. 1981, pp. 943–949.
45. *The Effect of the Method of Payment on Mental Health Care Practice*, Group for the Advancement of Psychiatry, 419 Park Avenue South, New York, 1975, pp. 629–633.
46. Ibid.

Bibliography

BASCH, MICHAEL FRANS, *Doing Psychotherapy*, Basic Books, New York, 1980.

BORENZWEIG, HERMAN, "Agency Versus Private Practice: Similarities and Differences," *Social Work*, May 1981, NASW, Washington, D.C.

DILLARD, ANNIE, *Pilgrim at Tinker Creek*, Bantam Books, New York, 1975.

The Effect of the Method of Payment on Mental Health Care Practice, Group for the Advancement of Psychiatry, 419 Park Avenue South, New York, 1975.

FIEDLER, F. E., "The Concept of an Ideal Therapeutic Relationship," *Journal of Consulting Psychology*, vol. 14, 1950, and "A Comparison of Therapeutic Relationships: Psychoanalytic, Non-directive, and Adlerian Therapy," *Journal of Consulting Psychology*, vol. 14, 1950.

FIZDALE, RUTH, "Formalizing the Relationship Between Private Practitioners and Social Agencies," *Social Casework*, Dec. 1959.

FIZDALE, RUTH, *Social Agency Structure and Accountability*, R. E. Burdick, Inc., Fair Haven, N.J. 07410, 1974.

FRANK, JEROME, "General Psychotherapy: The Restoration of Morale," in *American Handbook of Psychiatry*, Second Edition, Silvano Arieti, Editor-in-Chief,, Vol. 5, Daniel X. Freedman and J. Dyrud, Editors, Basic Books, New York, 1975.

FROMM-REICHMANN, FRIEDA, *Principles of Intensive Psychotherapy*, University of Chicago Press, Chicago, 1950.

"Guide to Private Practice," *Psychotherapy Finances*, Ridgewood Financial Institute, Inc., 75 Oak Street, Ridgewood, N.J., 1980.

HALMOS, PAUL, *The Faith of Counselors*, Schocken Books, New York, 1966.

HENRY, W. E., and SIMS, J., *The Fifth Profession: Becoming a Psychotherapist*, Jossey-Bass, San Francisco, 1971.

HOGAN, DANIEL B., *The Regulation of Psychotherapists*, Ballinger, Cambridge, Mass., 1979—particularly Vol. 2, *A Handbook of State Licensure Laws*.

JUNG, C. G., *Psychological Reflections: A New Anthology of His Writings, 1905-1961*, selected and edited by J. Jacobi with R. F. C. Hull, Princeton University Press, Princeton, N.J., 1970.

LEVIN, ARNOLD M. (Ed.), *Handbook on the Private Practice of Social Work*, revised, NASW, Washington, D.C., 1974.

LEVIN, ARNOLD M., "Private Practice Is Alive and Well," *Social Work*, vol. 21, No. 5, September 1976.

LEVIN, ARNOLD M., "See Me! Hear Me! Say My Name!" Unpublished paper, 1962.

LEVIN, ARNOLD M., "Social Workers in Mid-Career," unpublished doctoral dissertation, University of Chicago, August 1976.

LEVINSON, DANIEL J., *The Seasons of a Man's Life*, Knopf, New York, 1978.

LEVINSTEIN, SIDNEY, *Private Practice in Social Casework*, Columbia University Press, New York, 1964.

NACHT, S., LEBOVICI, S., and DIETKINE, R., "Training for Psychoanalysis,"*International Journal of Psychoanalysis*, vol. XLII, Parts 1-2, January-April, 1961.

NEUGARTEN, BERNICE L., *Middle Age and Aging*, University of Chicago Press, Chicago, 1968.

NEUGARTEN, BERNICE L., and DATAN, NANCY, "The Middle Years," *American Handbook of Psychiatry*, Second Edition, edited by Silvano Arieti, Basic Books, New York, 1975.

ORNE, MARTIN, "Psychotherapy in Contemporary America: Its Development and Context," in *American Handbook of Psychiatry*, Second Edition, Sylvano Arieti, Editor-in-Chief, Vol. 5, Basic Books, New York, 1975.

PERLMAN, HELEN HARRIS, "The Problem Solving Model in Social Casework," as cited in *Theories of Social Casework*, edited by Robert W. Roberts and Robert H. Knee, University of Chicago Press, Chicago, 1970.

QUINN, ROBERT P., STAINES, GRAHAM L., and McCULLOUGH, MARGARET R., *Job Satisfaction: Is There a Trend]* Manpower Research Monograph No. 30, U.S. Department of Labor, Washington, D.C., 1974.

RAIMY, V. C. (Ed.), *Training in Clinical Psychotherapy*, Prentice-Hall, Englewood Cliffs, N.J., 1950.

SHIMBERG, EDMUND, Ph.D., *The Handbook of Private Practice in Psychology*, Brunner/Mazel, New York, 1979.

SOBEL, DAVA, *New York Times Magazine*, Oct. 26, 1980.

TOWLE, CHARLOTTE, *The Learner in Education for the Professions*, University of Chicago Press, Chicago, 1954.

WALLACE, MARQUIS, "Autonomy in Private Practice," unpublished dissertation, University of Chicago, 1977.

Index